How to Invest

in

Sports Shares

How to Invest

in

Sports Shares

by

Benjamin Cooper

and

Andrew McHattie

B. T. BATSFORD LIMITED · LONDON

© Benjamin Cooper and Andrew McHattie 1997
First published 1997

Published by B T Batsford Ltd,
583 Fulham Road,
London SW6 5BY

Printed by
Redwood Books
Trowbridge
Wiltshire

ISBN 0 7134 8346 6

A CIP catalogue record for this book
is available from The British Library

HOW TO INVEST IN SPORTS SHARES

PREFACE

The world of soccer is never far away from the headlines and sports writers are seldom stuck for a story or an attention grabbing phrase. As the 'peoples game' it has everything to offer: drama, characters, passion, opinions, and always that vital ingredient, controversy.

But for the best part of a century the game barely progressed beyond the cloth cap image that was, at the same time, both its appeal and its ball and chain. Now, a series of unprecedented events have lifted football from its comfortable, generally outdated, existence and propelled it headlong towards a harder world where business can – and must – have the last word if professional clubs are to survive and prosper.

New grounds, better facilities, players' agents, freedom of contract, sponsorship, and TV deals have arrived, but not every club is geared to maximising its true potential.

I believe there are only about eighteen clubs who can do that by successful flotation on the Stock Market, a move Sheffield United made in January 1997.

It was a carefully calculated move which, as well as securing the future of the club through Sheffield United plc, gave our supporters their first and probably only opportunity to invest in their club – and see it on the financial pages as well as in the sports sections.

As a result the football club has a higher profile, ambitious but achievable targets and a position of strength that I think will encourage investors, private or otherwise, to consider the *new* world of football as worthy of consideration.

Charles Green
Chief Executive
Sheffield United plc

ACKNOWLEDGEMENTS

We are most grateful for the help of the following people and organisations, without whom this book could not have been written: Barron's, Nick Batram, Bloomberg, Tony Drury, Michael Goldman, Sarah King, Rachel Lockyer, John McHattie, Harold Nass, Rachel Norris, Martin Rands, and Reuters.

1

SPORTS SHARES ARE IN FASHION

Sport is pervasive. It is sending its tentacles out in all kinds of directions, including art (Michael Browne's Christ-like depiction of Eric Cantona, based on Piero della Francesca's *Resurrection of Christ* has caused a sensation at the Manchester City Art Gallery), music, film and literature (*Fever Pitch*), humour, computer games, expensive memorabilia (for keen football fans, a copy of the programme for England's 6-3 victory over Germany in Berlin in 1938 is worth around £350), and of course television.

Even education has now embraced the beautiful game, and at Oldborough Manor Community School in Maidstone, pupils can gain the equivalent of three 'A' levels by specialising in football. The school offers two GNVQs in business, centred on football, plus 'A' level PE. An obvious progression from there is to Liverpool University, which is starting an MBA in the football industry, after which you could join the centre for football research at Leicester University. Love it or hate it, sport is difficult to escape.

And for investors, sports shares have become an almost inescapable part of the scene. Sports shares are not only highly newsworthy, but they are often volatile in reaction to events, which means that they often feature in digests and reports. Few investors have failed to notice that Manchester United is a stock market listed company.

The sector is dominated by soccer, both in terms of profile and activity, but is actually more varied than is usually realised. Britain can lay claim to being at least the runner-up to America in the sporting investment stakes, and boasts a rapidly growing sector. In the last six months alone there have been at least 15 new issues in the field, with many more to come. A Reuters listing for forthcoming new issues on the London Stock Exchange, posted in April 1997, bears testimony to the current popularity of sports shares. No fewer than seven out of 31 new issues (23%) were sports shares, ranking it first by sector.

A DEFINITION OF SPORTS SHARES

So what exactly is a sports share? Any definition is bound to be woolly around the edges, but for the purposes of this book any company which has sports-related operations as a substantial part of its overall business is included. There is a whole host of companies which have minor interests and are excluded, but plenty which are truly specialist. Readers may be surprised at just how many stock exchange listed companies are active in the field, many of which are hidden behind anonymous corporate exteriors.

Grampian Holdings is the manufacturer of Penfold golf balls; Windsor is an international sports insurance broker; Sunleigh makes sporting boats and the 'PowaKaddy' golf cart; and there are dozens more companies operating in peripheral areas. Many sports companies can boast well-known brands and products which are perhaps little appreciated by investors at large.

Table 1.1: a selection of sports brands

Brand / Product	Company
'Megabowl' bowling centres	Allied Leisure
'First Sport' shops	Blacks Leisure Group
'ActiveVenture' shops	Blacks Leisure Group
'Ben Sayers' golf clubs	Grampian Holdings
'Admiral' football strips	Hay & Robertson
'Premier PJ's' football nightwear	Hay & Robertson
'Mitre' sports footwear	Pentland Group
'Speedo' swimwear	Pentland Group
'Ellesse' sportswear	Pentland Group
'Ralgex' muscular relief	Seton Healthcare
'Sondico' goalkeeping gloves	Seton Healthcare
'Laser' and 'Dart' yachts	Sunleigh

The ability to recognise products is important, because most investors like to invest in companies which they can follow; usually where there is a strong element of observational judgement. In other words, where you have a chance to see for yourself how the company is doing. This is certainly true for a wide range of sports shares. You can see for yourself how individual football clubs are performing; you can see how different sports shops present their goods; you can see whether betting shops are becoming more friendly and attractive.

WHY CONSIDER INVESTING IN SPORTS SHARES?

No one said that investment should not be fun. Sports shares provide the opportunity to combine serious investment and money-making with a sector which is great fun to follow. Your hobbies can become investments, and better than that, they can turn investment itself into a sport, a hobby, a pastime. This is why the sports share sector carries an irresistible attraction for many investors tired of dull companies making products which are of no particular interest. Other sectors such as technology, smaller companies, and investment trusts all have their devotees, but for sheer appeal sports shares are hard to beat.

For newspaper readers who start reading their papers from the back, it can even justify the time spent considering the prospects for Newcastle United's season, or whether Adidas are still making their shirts. Such is the interest in sports shares that some journalists are finding the borders between sport and finance increasingly blurred. There is an expanding amount of coverage in the press for sports shares and the commercial aspects of leisure.

Journalists such as Jason Nissé of *The Times* and Mihir Bose of *The Daily Telegraph* have specialised in this field, and even *The Financial Times* now runs a 'Business of Sport' section every Friday. Beyond these regular news items, there is an investment newsletter – *Sports Shares* – devoted to the sector, plus reports from stockbrokers and accountants.

WHY NOW?

As Nomura International stated in a document in 1996: "Football clubs, as an area of investment are no longer simply reserved for romantic fans and loyal game followers, but have become a lucrative area for investors of all types." Football clubs have been the spur for the sector, and appropriately, it was Spurs which started it all.

Tottenham Hostpur was the first football club to be listed in London back in 1983, and it was not regarded as being of investment grade at the time. Football clubs were just an amusing distraction from the real business of the stockmarket, and analysts denied that clubs had any true investment worth. Beyond a share certificate for fans to frame above the mantelpiece, football club shares were best avoided, according to the conventional wisdom. It is difficult to overstate the extent of the revolution which has since occurred. Consider the following extracts from an article which appeared in the *Investors Chronicle*:

- *"Football has always enjoyed a traditionally British approach to sport: as long as it's fun it does not have to make money."*

- *"There is little direct contact between football and the City."*

- *"League clubs have poor finances – a report a couple of years ago found 80 of the 92 League clubs technically insolvent."*

- *"The Italians have spent more than £500m on their stadia for the World Cup. Such sums are beyond the ken of the British game, despite the help of the private sector."*

Was this written in 1970? 1980? Actually, as the World Cup clue may have given away, it was in the *Investors Chronicle* of 1 June 1990, when only Tottenham Hotspur, Millwall and Edinburgh Hibernian were quoted clubs. Since then, a revolution has occurred, football club shares have multiplied in value, proliferated in number, and attracted a crowd of delighted investors. The massive, largely unexpected, success of the sector is discussed in Chapter 2, and the key influence of television in Chapter 3.

The rest of the quoted sports sector, which is now quite extensive, is discussed in Chapter 4. Just as there is now a broad range of sports companies in which to invest, there are varying methods of choosing the right ones (Chapter 5) and varying ways of using your capital (Chapter 6). You can even venture overseas, and Chapter 7 explains how many sports businesses are well established in all kinds of niches, in America in particular. Chapter 8 concludes with a look to the future.

Sport is a huge commercial arena now, and that is an undisputable fact. For people who believe that the increasing element of overt commercialisation in sport is ruining its core principles, that football referees should wear black and tennis players should wear white, the passing of an era may be mourned. For most people though, the commercial revolution means more sport, of a higher quality, to be viewed in safety and comfort. The 'money men' receive their slice, certainly, but you too can buy a share. This book explains how.

2

CHAPTER TWO – FOOTBALL CLUBS

Football has become big business. In April 1995 the number of listed football clubs could be counted on the fingers of one hand. Manchester United and Tottenham Hotspur headed the table in market capitalisation with 'tiddlers' Preston North End and Millwall way behind. Since then the City has fallen in love with the concept and persuaded many others to join the fold. By April 1997 the number of clubs listed on the AIM, OFEX, or with full listings, had increased to 23 as the lure of financial gain for the directors, development capital for the stadium, and funds for new team signings had attracted clubs to the stockmarket.

Such is the support in the City for soccer club flotations that Dale Thorpe, a football industry analyst at accountants Deloitte & Touche, reckons that football teams are viable long-term investments and that "we'll probably see all the Premier League clubs listed either on the main market or on the AIM in the next few years". For investors, the key attraction lies in the stunning performance of shares such as Manchester United, which jumped from 126p in January 1995 to a high of 738p two years later – a rise of 481%.

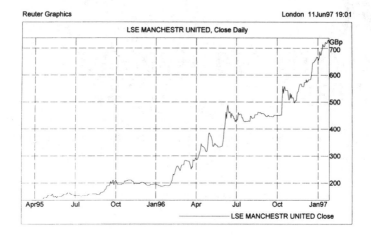

Figure 2.1: Manchester United Share Price 1995-1997
(source: Reuters)

But what has driven these clubs to their current valuations? And why may a particular club be headed higher still? Or what might make you think a particular club is not a good investment? This chapter takes a look at listed football clubs, compares the different methods of producing revenue, analyses the reasons a club may decide to float on the stockmarket, and highlights some of the pitfalls you need to avoid.

THE FOOTBALL BUSINESS

Football clubs have come a long way from their image of cold steak pies on a dreary Saturday afternoon with the cigar smoking, camel hair coated club chairman attempting to live out a boyhood dream. Football clubs have shaken off their amateur image and many have been developed into sports and leisure companies aimed at family entertainment. They are exploiting their brand image and, some might argue, their fans. A modern football club's revenue stream has become a winding, complex system and the number of ways a club can produce revenue may come as a surprise. The revenue of most clubs can be divided into seven main areas: (i) gate receipts; (ii) merchandising; (iii) sponsorship; (iv) competition earnings; (v) transfer income; (vi) television; and (vii) other sports related activities.

GATE RECEIPTS

According to stockbroker Greig Middleton's *Football Industry Review 1997*, attendances at English football games in the1949/1950 season reached 40m people. This figure declined substantially over the next 36 years when, in the 1985/86 season, total attendances fell to a low of 16.5m – a 60% drop. The decline was arguably brought on by a change in working habits, an increase in alternative leisure activities, and in the 1970s and early 1980s, the advent of hooliganism. The threat of violence caused many to stay away from football games, particularly those supporters with children. In the 1984/85 season the police made over 7,000 arrests from a total attendance of 18m. Hooliganism also reduced the success of clubs in Europe, as following the death of Italian fans at a Liverpool versus Juventus tie in the Heysel Stadium, a ban prevented English clubs from participating in European competition. This reduced English football's exposure in the media, particularly abroad, and it became extremely difficult to attract foreign players who wished to play on the larger stage of European football.

Following the 1985/86 season, attendances at football games began to grow again and this has continued steadily over the past decade. In the 1994/95 season attendances had risen to 21.3m and the number of arrests had fallen by 50% to under 4,000. More importantly, the quality of earnings had also improved. The traditional area of support for football had been from the C2 or lower economic bands, and principally male. However, a report published by Leicester University in November 1996 showed supporters were becoming increasingly sophisticated. According to its findings, 36.8% of Manchester United and 34.6% of Leeds United season ticket holders have degrees and a growing number of fans earn salaries which exceed £30,000 a year. The number of female supporters has also increased to one in eight and, the report claims, the number is rising rapidly.

Two key legal factors have also helped pave the way for the steady increase in attendances. The 1990 Taylor Report was produced following the Hillsborough tragedy which claimed the lives of 92 Liverpool fans at an FA Cup semi-final in Sheffield. The report suggested many improvements to football stadium safety, but the major proposal was the introduction of all-seater grounds. Subsequently, Premiership and First Division football clubs were required to convert to all-seater stadiums by the start of the 1994/95 season. Many clubs had to invest large sums of money in ground improvements and this has produced safer, cleaner, and more comfortable stadiums for supporters. The investment programme has continued throughout the past six seasons and looks set to continue as smaller clubs upgrade their facilities. The second factor is more recent. In 1996, Jean-Marc Bosman took European football's governing body, UEFA, to the European Court and won. Bosman fought against a ruling which meant, despite being out of contract, a player could not move to another club within the EU, but outside his domestic league, without a transfer fee being paid. The result brought a change in UEFA's rules concerning foreign players and an influx of out-of-contract international 'stars' into the English and Scottish Leagues.

The effect on the revenue football clubs earn from gate receipts has been dramatic, particularly in the English Premier League. The introduction of newer facilities, foreign stars and a change of image has allowed many clubs to pass increased costs on to spectators who are prepared to pay a premium price. Greig Middleton's report suggests that despite a modest 20% increase in attendances, the value of gate receipts in the English league nearly quadrupled between the 1984/85 and the 1994/95 seasons. However, the danger is that supporters may reach a plateau in the amount they are prepared to pay to watch a game. A survey by research group Mintel in November 1996 showed that as many as 33% of soccer supporters felt they were being 'ripped off' by their clubs. Many clubs may be reaching a revenue ceiling which could place a brake on future growth in gate money. The industry is however a step ahead, and many clubs have developed other operations which produce a larger proportion of total income each season.

MERCHANDISING

Merchandising was, for a long time, an under-developed area of the soccer industry. Clubs introduced, annually, a home and away kit which was replicated by the kit supplier and sold to the team's fans. Other products such as bobble-hats, scarves and mugs were also produced which enabled supporters to be recognised. In recent years as the game has become increasingly commercialised, so the clubs have begun to exploit fans' loyalty by developing a wider range of products, branded with team colours and motif. This type of 'brand management' is clearly illustrated by one of the strongest soccer brands in the world – Manchester United. In 1991, the year of its stockmarket flotation, Manchester United generated revenue, minus gate receipts, of £8.6m which represented 48% of total sales. During the 1996 financial year, Manchester United increased this figure to £34.6m, some 65% of total income. The club managed to do this by introducing a range of new kits each season, along with the facility to have favourite players' names and numbers printed on the back. The club shop introduced a much wider range of branded products including books, videos, casual wear, drinks, food and even affiliated bank accounts and credit cards. Manchester United also has a well-developed ground offering executive boxes, catering and licensed bars and restaurants for supporters. While this amount of commercial potential may be limited to the major Premier League sides, the example clearly shows how merchandising has become a major factor in the business of running a successful football team, and how having a strong commercial sense has helped develop clubs into businesses.

Brand image is an important strength in marketing, and the key advantage for a football team is the loyalty towards it. As football supporters will tell you, their allegiances rarely change, and if adopted early enough, a child can become a potential supporter – and client – for the rest of his or her life. Another advantage is the extensive press coverage which football clubs receive. A club has to spend very little on advertising when they appear in the newspapers and on the television almost daily. Clubs are developing an increasing array of branded products to sell to supporters and this area of the business has increasingly begun to outstrip the revenue produced by the actual game on a Saturday afternoon.

SPONSORSHIP

Football clubs have high profile images both locally and nationally. The high levels of press and television coverage each team receives has not only been exploited by the club itself, but by other product producers. Sponsorship can be broken down into four key areas: (i) kit sponsorship; (ii) shirt sponsorship; (iii) ground sponsorship; and (iv) game sponsorship.

Sportswear has become a major area of the fashion clothing world, as you will see in Chapter 4, and football kit producers aim to take advantage of this by sponsoring football club kits. A major kit manufacturer will pay a large amount of money to supply a team with its kit each season just to enable them to sell replica shirts to the club's supporters – sales from which the club also receives a percentage. Umbro, the largest supplier of football kits in England, currently has a six year deal with Manchester United, reportedly worth £40m.

Other companies are also keen to have their products endorsed by football clubs. This normally involves shirt sponsorship where a company buys the exclusive right to have its name or logo printed on the team's shirt. For a Premiership side, national companies are often interested, such as JVC for Arsenal, Sharp for Manchester United, and Scottish & Newcastle for Newcastle United. The lower division clubs tend to attract more local businesses, such as Eddie Stobart for Carlisle United. Again, the sums of money paid for this honour can boost revenue significantly. Chelsea's new shirt contract with Autoglass is reportedly worth £4.5m over the next four years. Large companies also pay huge amounts of money to sponsor entire leagues. Carling recently renewed its four year contract with the Premier League, tripling the amount paid to £36m for the seasons 1997/98 to 2000/01. Carling reportedly fought off competition from British Telecom and Ford. The money is distributed equally among the clubs, at £450,000 per team, per season.

It has been traditional at football grounds for local and national companies to take advantage of a captive audience by placing advertising hoardings around the perimeter of the pitch. In recent seasons the practice has been improved with the introduction of revolving hoardings which allow several companies to use each space around the ground, thereby increasing revenue for the club. Also, in recent years, companies have taken advantage of the increased level of building work and renovations at stadiums to sponsor the construction of new stands. Middlesborough's new Riverside Stadium is sponsored by Cellnet, Bristol City's new Atteyo stand is sponsored by Carling, Huddersfield's futuristic new ground is called the Alfred McAlpine Stadium, and Bolton Wanderers have been paid £2m by Reebok to lend its name to the new stadium.

On matchdays, teams often have sponsors for the game, the ball, and even individual items of a player's kit. The cost varies enormously between clubs and divisions, but again, it is a valuable source of income. For example, companies wishing to sponsor Leeds United's match ball will have to fork out £500 for the honour, and for a 'full sponsorship pack' should set aside at least £3,250.

MULTI-PURPOSE FACILITIES

A football team's ground is its spiritual home, but it can also be its most underutilised asset. The ground stands empty in the off-season and when the team plays away, only producing revenue when the team is at home, which could be as few as twenty times each season for a Premier League side. Many clubs have now begun to use their grounds in a number of ways to produce alternative revenue when football is not being played. Conference facilities, restaurants, and bars are now common, and a few others, including Chelsea, intend to redevelop the surrounding areas to offer leisure and hotel facilities.

Another growing trend is the introduction of ground sharing. Loftus Road, owners of Queen's Park Rangers Football Club and the Wasps Rugby Union side, was the first listed company to stage both Premier League football and First Division rugby at its Loftus Road stadium. Others have now followed, with Preston North End acquiring a Rugby League side to play at its Deepdale stadium in the summer months, and Caspian, owners of Leeds United, acquiring the franchise for an ice hockey team to play at an ice rink to be built alongside the Elland Road ground. Other clubs are also teaming up with third party developers and moving to out-of-town sites which combine the attractions of a new all-seater stadium with other leisure facilities such as cinemas, bowling alleys and hotel accommodation.

TRANSFER INCOME

The transfer market involves the buying and selling of players' contracts, and can be a regular source of income for some clubs. Since the Bosman ruling, any European player operating within the European Union has the right to a free transfer to a team in a different European Union member country, as long as his contract has expired. At present, the same rule does not apply to out-of-contract players moving between teams within the same country, but this is likely to be challenged in the European Courts in the very near future following Newcastle United's signing of Blackburn Rovers out-of-contract goalkeeper Shay Given. The two teams failed to agree on a transfer fee and in normal circumstances the deal would go to an independent tribunal to decide a fair fee. However, Newcastle "proposes to raise this [the Bosman] issue before the independent tribunal," and a legal challenge can be expected should the tribunal disagree with Newcastle. The outcome of such a challenge will probably lead to the law, which allows freedom of movement of workers within the EU, becoming applicable within domestic leagues.

At present, clubs sign players to contracts to play for their teams. Contracts can be for any length of time, but are normally around three years. During this period, should another team become interested in the player for their own squad the new team must make an offer to the present team to buy out the player's present contract. The most famous transfer in recent English soccer history was England team captain Alan Shearer's £15m move from Blackburn Rovers to Newcastle United in the summer of 1996. At the time the move broke all soccer transfer records. Brazilian star Ronaldo is expected to break the record by signing for Italian giants Inter Milan, from Spain's European Cup Winners Cup champions, Barcelona, for a reported £19m. For lower division clubs the transfer market is an extremely important revenue producer which helps them to stay operational. Clubs such as Charlton Athletic, which listed on the AIM in March 1997, have a tradition of developing exceptional young talents, signing them to contracts, and then selling them on to big clubs for large sums of money. Midfielder Lee Bowyer was signed by Leeds United for £2.6m in July 1996 which, at the time, made Lee the most expensive teenager in English football history.

The Bosman case has made the future for clubs dependant on transfer income slightly more uncertain. The big clubs in English football have now taken to signing foreign 'star' players on free transfers, rather than buying young, contracted players from lower division clubs. The stars bring instant appeal, draw supporters, and can bring instant success – but they do command high salaries as a result.

TELEVISION REVENUE

The major driving force behind the impressive share price performances of football clubs has been the potential value of television revenue. The introduction of a new four year contract, starting with the 1997/98 season, for Premier League matches has increased the value of clubs' television revenue as much as five fold. BSkyB has also agreed a five year deal ending in 2001 with the three lower divisions, but the amounts are not comparable. The inevitable introduction of digital television and pay-per-view has the City analysts grabbing for their calculators as they attempt to value the possible incomes many of the Premier League clubs could receive. The development of television is such an important factor in the business of football, and other sports, that we have devoted Chapter 3 to the subject.

OTHER ACTIVITIES

To survive as businesses, many clubs are now recognising the need to develop beyond their traditional sporting activities. While the success of the team is normally the main concern for the board of the company, this is often to help bank-roll expansion into other areas. Caspian, the owners of Leeds United, is an excellent example of a company looking beyond its 'bread-and-butter' football club and planning to become, as chairman Chris Akers describes it, "a sports, leisure and media group." Caspian has already acquired Leeds Ice Hockey Club and negotiated its inclusion in the Ice Hockey Super League (ISL), starting with the 1998/99 season. Ice hockey is one of the fastest growing sports in the UK, and Caspian intends to take full advantage of this by building an ice rink on the Elland Road site, adjacent to the football ground. Caspian's proposal also includes a multi-purpose arena capable of hosting concerts, exhibitions, extensive hospitality events and basketball – another fast growing spectator sport.

Chelsea Village is another football company with plans for alternative revenue production, but this does not involve the introduction of other sports to Stamford Bridge. Chelsea's plan involves the redevelopment of the land surrounding Stamford Bridge in the highly fashionable Chelsea area of London. The company is already building apartments which it plans to sell for premium prices, but the major project is a 160-room hotel – the 'Chelsea Village'. Special rates will be offered when Chelsea play at home, which should help iron out the hotel's earnings which, in the industry, usually fall flat during the winter months.

COSTS

As clubs earn increasing amounts of money from their football related activities, so the costs of running such operations also increase. The most notable rise is in players' wages. Ultimately, it is the players on the pitch who produce the success on which the company builds its business, and they are the ones the fans idolise. It is perhaps not surprising that the idols have begun to demand a larger slice of the revenue.

Players' wages have increased in excess of inflation since 1990, and have accelerated over the past two seasons since the result of the Bosman case. As the future of players' movements has become an increasingly grey area, clubs with talented players have attempted to tie them to longer contracts, reducing the chance of them moving abroad on a free transfer at the end of their contract, and increasing the possibility of obtaining a transfer fee should another club wish to acquire the player. The problem with this tactic is that players wish to be compensated for the reduction of their future options, and this can have a major impact on a club's wage bill. Tottenham Hotspur, a club with an image of tough cost control, saw its wage bill increase by £1m, or 13%, in the first half of the 1996/97 financial year following the signing of four new players and the renegotiation of a number of key players' contracts.

The Bosman ruling has also affected the wage bills of some of the larger clubs due to the signing of out-of-contract foreign stars. Chelsea Village has taken the greatest advantage of the new freedom in player movement by creating a cosmopolitan team of European players including Lebouef, Di Matteo, Vialli, and Zola. The benefit is that the players arrived either on free transfers, or their clubs accepted smaller transfer fees because of the short period of time remaining on their contracts. The cost is the enormous wages these players are paid. Players such as Vialli are rumoured to command salaries in excess of £20,000 per week. These costs need to be met, and teams are increasing the prices of merchandise and seats to cover them.

WHY COME TO THE STOCKMARKET?

With just four listed clubs in April 1995, you might ask why the number has risen four-fold, with the majority arriving in the latter part of 1996 and first half of 1997. The simple and common answer, you may have guessed, is money. What varies is how each club uses the money, and this can often determine which clubs are of investment grade, and worthy of consideration for your portfolio, or simply fan grade, and worth little to those outside the club's supporter base.

The main reason most clubs wish to raise additional finance is to improve their chances of, or to prepare themselves for, inclusion in the Premier League. The Premier League is the top echelon of English soccer, and its clubs earn by far the most revenue. Clubs which already compete in the Premier League may wish to raise additional capital to cash in on their status and, more importantly, maintain their position. With three teams relegated to the Nationwide First Division each season, the desire to do well in the top flight is driven not only by pride, but by money too.

HOW ARE FUNDS RAISED?

To finance improvements in the stadium, team, or other operation, a football club has a number of options. For years the main option has been bank financing and/or the injection of capital by a wealthy benefactor. Blackburn Rovers, Chelsea Village and Newcastle United are three famous beneficiaries of cash injections by wealthy businessmen. Jack Walker, a self-made millionaire, invested a huge sum in Blackburn, buying them top players to enable promotion to the Premier League, and subsequently the Championship. For many of the lower division clubs this type of financing remains the only way of raising the capital required for major expansion. For the larger, more fashionable clubs, however, the stockmarket is like a light to a moth.

The most recognised route to the stockmarket for any company, be it an engineering business or a football club, is by flotation. This involves the issue of shares in the company at a predetermined price. The club can raise the capital entirely from institutions, through a placing of shares, or allow the public, and particularly supporters, an opportunity to buy some shares in the club, via an offer for sale. The issues are normally underwritten, guaranteeing the sale of all the shares on offer. This allows the club to determine how much the company is to be valued at and how much money is to be raised by the placing and offer. For example, the flotation of Newcastle United involved a placing and open offer of 40m shares, or 28% of the company, at 135p per share. The flotation raised £54m for Newcastle United and valued the club at £193m. Unfortunately for many supporters, the majority of football clubs seeking listings appear to forget their fans when the ownership of the club is up for grabs, and simply place all the shares with institutions. The only way to gain access is by buying shares in the market once they begin trading, a process discussed in Chapter 6.

Often, the flotation of a football club has brought an instant profit to those involved in the initial offer. A good example is Sunderland Football Club. Sunderland shares were offered to investors at 585p per share in December 1996, to fund the construction of a new stadium and to strengthen the team. The offer was oversubscribed by 2.7 times and on the first day of trading the shares jumped to 740p – a 25% premium to the offer price.

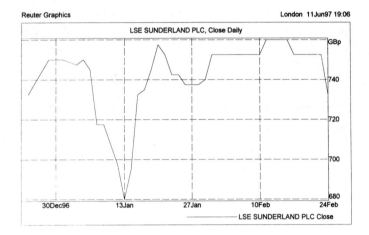

Figure 2.2 Sunderland Football Club Share Price 1996/97
(source: *Sports Shares*)

More recently, another method of obtaining a stockmarket listing has been utilised. It is technically called a reversal, and involves the club using an existing moribund company with a Stock Exchange listing – a shell – as its vehicle. This has been used on a number of occasions, including Southampton Football Club's reversal into Secure Retirement, Sheffield United's reversal into Conrad, and Bolton Wanderers' reversal into Mosaic Investments (now Burnden Leisure). The deal involves the shell acquiring the football club by issuing a huge number of new shares to the owners of the football club. The result is that the owners of the club now hold a large percentage of the enlarged capital of the shell company, giving them overall control. This can prove cheaper than a direct flotation, and in some circumstances it can be a canny way to delay a cash-raising exercise until the funds are actually required. For shareholders of the shell company it invariably provides a boost to the share price (usually after a period of suspension), so if the deal is carefully structured it can be of benefit to all participants.

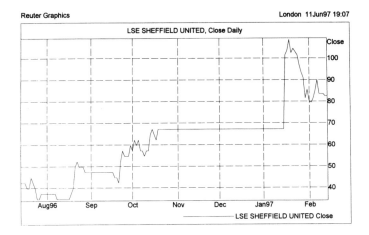

Figure 2.3 Conrad/Sheffield United Share Price 1996/97
(source: Reuters)

Whichever way a club chooses to obtain a stockmarket listing, the
ability to invest in its future is an attractive prospect for many private
investors. The historic returns of listed football clubs has been
impressive and although the past returns are not necessarily a guide to
the future, the potential of a well run football club with a good chance
to remain in, or gain access to, the Premier League can be huge.

HOW ARE THE ADDITIONAL FUNDS USED?

The desire for a football club to play in the lucrative Premier League
must be supported by its playing and managerial staff, and to
construct a side of Premier League quality can be an expensive
business. The majority of football clubs which list on the
stockmarket earmark a proportion of the funds raised to strengthen
the team, or to pay back debts which had been built up in acquiring
new talent. Clubs such as Newcastle United and Chelsea are famous
for constructing their teams around expensive foreign imports, and

the money raised in their flotations has been used to repay or fund those acquisitions.

The area which attracts the majority of funds raised, however, is the improvement or construction of stadium facilities. All the clubs which have raised money on the stockmarket have done so, principally, to improve their grounds, be it the construction of a new stand, redevelopment of an existing one, or the construction of an entirely new stadium. In the past, improvements required to stadia, as directed by the Taylor Report, were financed with the help of The Football Trust. The Trust provides finance for the development of football in the UK and is financed, principally, by the pools companies which supply around 85% of the money raised. The majority of the money raised has been directed to clubs in the top two divisions to help with the improvements required by the Taylor Report. Recently, however, the money raised by the Trust has declined, largely as a result of the introduction of the National Lottery. This has cut the size and number of grants given by the Trust, thereby amplifying the need for clubs to raise money on the stockmarket. The reduction in funds from the Football Trust could be particularly damaging for smaller clubs as it is this second part of the plan, to help finance smaller clubs' stadium plans, which is now coming to the fore. One possible result is an increasing number of smaller clubs listing on the AIM. Sadly, most of these smaller club shares will be of interest to fans only, although those wishing to widen their shareholder base should take heart from Preston North End which came to the market as a Third Division club and has been run impressively, attracting praise and support from the City.

Finally, funds are sometimes used for lateral expansion. The listing of Chelsea Village, owners of Chelsea Football Club, was as much about the board's plans to redevelop the area surrounding the Stamford Bridge stadium, as it was about the team itself. For Preston North End, the majority of the funds were directed towards the construction of the Tom Finney stand, but the club also had plans to acquire a Rugby League side to play at the Deepdale stadium during the summer months and to provide the right image to attract FIFA's new Soccer Museum – which has now been given the go-ahead. It is important to the success of any company to have plans for expansion and diversification and this also applies to football clubs.

THE RISKS

With all stockmarket investment there is risk, and one particular story has brought the football industry down to earth. Millwall came to the market in 1989 with an offer for sale at 20p at a time when the club was enjoying a spell in the top flight. Over the following seasons the club raised additional cash to finance the construction of a new stadium, the New Den. The team, however, slipped a division and the share price slipped with them until in April 1992 the shares hit an all-time low of 1.75p, some 93.7% below the original issue price. Despite a strong first half of the season in 1995/96, which saw them challenging for promotion, the team experienced a run of form which saw the club enter free-fall in the league table and they were subsequently relegated to the Second Division. At this point the cost base of the club had been geared up for Premiership football – and Premiership income – but now had to face Second Division attendances and a second rate level of revenue. The club attempted to reduce costs, but on 21st January 1997 the directors decided to have the shares suspended at just 4p and called in the administrators, leaving the club approximately £10m in debt.

Despite this tarnish to the sector, important lessons can be learnt from the demise of Millwall. The key lesson is that stock selection is important. You cannot invest in the football sector in general and hope for homogeneous returns. The major risk is that the performance of a squad of players on a field can determine the current and potential earnings of a football club. The difference in television revenue (see Chapter 3) between the clubs in the Premier League and those in the First Division is enormous, and the level of merchandising, gate receipts and sponsorship are also all geared for the Premiership. Any club due to be promoted to the Premier League can expect a substantial rise in its share price, and the reverse is true for clubs facing relegation.

Another problem facing the industry is the potential for wage costs to spiral upwards. The Bosman ruling is likely to apply to domestic transfers in the very near future, and this could have a detrimental affect both on smaller clubs which depend on transfer income, and on larger clubs which are forced to pay players substantially higher wages. The situation will need to be monitored closely to identify the full impact.

CONCLUSION

The general consensus amongst City analysts and newspaper pundits is that there is a widening gap between the large Premier League clubs and those smaller clubs operating both in and out of the Premier League. As the big clubs increase their proportion of television revenue and improve their merchandising arms, the smaller clubs have to make a number of decisions. The most important one is to make themselves profitable on a smaller scale, and to avoid 'going-for-broke' to achieve promotion. Their model should be Preston North End which has Premiership aspirations, but is a well managed club with realistic short-term ambitions. Only a few clubs have the potential to challenge Manchester United as a business and the sooner many clubs realise this, the less chance we will witness another Millwall.

3

CHAPTER THREE – TELEVISION

Television has the ability to make or break sports. Look at snooker, which thanks to television has become the perfect armchair sport. Audiences are huge, and star players now command enormous prize earnings. Football may be different – it has always been the national game – but a hefty proportion of revenue for leading clubs now comes from exclusive broadcasting rights. Television, through satellite broadcasting companies especially, is dishing out large sums of cash, but in return it wants to make the rules. This is why Premier League matches are now played on virtually every day of the week.

In this chapter we concentrate on the changes in the broadcasting of sport, the effect it has had and might have on the football industry, and finally the potential many other sports have in broadcasting.

TERRESTRIAL TELEVISION

Before the introduction of satellite subscription channels Sky TV and British Satellite Broadcasting, which in 1990 merged to become BSkyB, the British viewing public were treated to just four channels – only two of which were 'mainstream' channels. The public were safe and comfortable in the knowledge that all the major sporting events both nationally and internationally would be broadcast – often live – to them in their living rooms via terrestrial television, and for only the cost of a licence fee. The low level of competition for sporting events meant that the two channels were unwilling to enter bidding wars to secure the rights for First Division football or any other major sport, and this left each sport with little 'muscle' to negotiate its own television deals. In the early 1980s, BBC and ITV collaborated to provide both live and highlighted soccer for two years for just £5.2m, and repeated the process in 1986, increasing the amount paid by just

19% to £6.2m. This deal gave the channels exclusive rights to all English league football games, and removed any form of competition that may have existed between the channels.

SATELLITE BROADCASTING

In 1988 the story changed for football and the ball began to roll for many other sports. At the end of BBC and ITV's two year contract, signed in 1986, Sky entered the arena for sports in an attempt to boost its limited subscription levels. The result was a bidding war, which was exactly what football clubs had been after for many years. The outcome was that football coverage was split between two parties. ITV secured the rights to live action from the Football League for four years in a deal worth £55m, a 340% *pro rata* rise on the previous contract. The BBC teamed up with Sky and ended their duopoly with ITV, a move which has since proved to be a significant event in the development and changing face of English football. The BBC/Sky joint venture purchased the rights from The Football Association for the FA Cup and all of the national team's games for five years at a cost of £30m.

The saga continued in 1990 when Sky TV and BSB merged to form BSkyB – a broadcaster with the financial muscle Sky lacked when competing with ITV for the 1988 deal to secure exclusive rights to league soccer. At this point, and after a successful World Cup competition in Italy, the top clubs in English football had begun to recognise the commercial potential of the game, and the next major step in the development of football coincided with the end of ITV's 1988-1992 contract. In 1992 the top clubs in England broke away from the Football League and created their own Premier League. This league contained the cream of English football, including Manchester United, Liverpool, Arsenal, Leeds United, Aston Villa and Chelsea. This gave the new league, which maintains an affiliation with the Football League, greater bargaining power in the ensuing television negotiations.

The negotiations for a new contract began in the same year and the Premier League secured a £304m five-year deal with BSkyB to show live games and with the BBC to show edited highlights. This represented another 340% increase in the value of the previous contract and now covered just the one top division. Remember that six years earlier the overall deal was worth just £6.2m – a shade over one-fiftieth of the 1992 sum. The new deal also calmed the Premier League's fears of over-exposure on television affecting the size of crowds at home games. The substantially smaller number of viewers watching games on 'Sky Sports' helped convince the Premier League to sign the deal. The deal was divided into three parts, with a basic award of 50% of each year's payment divided equally between each club in the Premier League; 25% allocated as a merit award determined by the final position of each club each season; and the remaining 25% was allocated for game fees for each match televised. This massively increased level of income from television revolutionised the way many of the football clubs were run, with Manchester United, the 1995/96 Premier League champions, receiving almost £3m from the BSkyB contract in that season alone.

THE CURRENT BSKYB PREMIER LEAGUE CONTRACT

The attractiveness of football continued to grow, and as the end of the BSkyB/BBC contract in 1997 came nearer, so the competition to secure television coverage into the next millennium became intense. Two new consortia – one led by United News and Media and another which included Carlton Communications and Mirror Group Newspapers – joined the fray and this pushed the value of the exclusive rights up significantly. There were three key factors which put BSkyB's £670m four-year deal in the clear. BSkyB's collaboration with the BBC provided some terrestrial exposure for the game, an option to review the contract after two years gave the Premier League greater flexibility, and the deal included an immediate £50m increase in the value of the final year of the current contract.

The new contract also included a £73m payment from the BBC for the edited highlights of Premier League games which took the total value of the deal to £743m – a 200% *pro rata* increase on the previous contract. The new deal, which begins with the 1997/98 season, is similar in construction to the 1992-97 contract, but the amounts are significantly higher. In the 1997/98 season each Premier League club should receive in the region of £3.7m for the basic payment; £200,000 for each place as a merit award; and as much as £350,000 per live game televised. For a team such as Manchester United, who might repeat their 1995/96 performance, the deal could result in a total payment for the 1997/98 season of around £12m from the BSkyB deal alone. For those Premier League teams with less chance of success, the minimum amount they could receive is almost £5m, more than Manchester United received in 1996 for winning the Premier League title. The BSkyB deal also includes 'parachute payments' for those unfortunate clubs which are relegated. These payments are equal to half the basic award, for a total of two seasons. This is in addition to the payments they are entitled to under the BSkyB contract for televising games in English divisions one to three, outlined below. This provides those clubs which have been relegated during the past three seasons, including Queen's Park Rangers (Loftus Road) and Sunderland, and those which are relegated during the 1997/98 to 2000/01 seasons with a substantial financial advantage to those attempting to gain promotion without these additional funds (such as Charlton Athletic, Birmingham City and West Bromwich Albion).

THE CURRENT BSKYB FOOTBALL LEAGUE CONTRACT

In June 1996 BSkyB completed its dominance of live English football by signing a deal with the English Football League, which is responsible for divisions one to three. This deal replaced the contract with the ITV network and was worth £125m over five years. The contract guaranteed each division one team with a payment of £620,000 per season, payable in twelve monthly instalments; a merit award of £11,000 for each position a team finishes above last place (with a minimum of £11,000 for last place). It also includes a game fee of £40,000 for each home team and £20,000 for each away team broadcast live on Sky Sports.

A First Division club with no Premier League involvement in the past two years can therefore earn around £870,000 for a mid-table performance with the equivalent of three home televised games. This is substantially less than the minimum earnings for a Premier League club facing relegation, and approximately £1.9m less than a relegated Premier League club attempting to regain promotion. It is little wonder, then, that First Division clubs seem so desperate for promotion, and are willing to spend heavily to attain it.

OTHER FOOTBALL TELEVISION CONTRACTS

Scottish football is a poor cousin to the English Premier League. The Scottish Premier League is normally contested between two clubs, Glasgow Rangers and Glasgow Celtic, and outside the top three or four clubs, the remainder would struggle against the corresponding English league sides. The lower quality of football and the substantially lower potential national audience for the majority of Scottish League games means the clubs have to accept a much reduced level of television revenue. The present four-year deal between the Scottish Football Association and the BSkyB/BBC/STV consortium, which expires at the end of the 1997/98 season, is worth just £16m. The Scottish Premier League expects the next contract to be significantly more rewarding, but it is unlikely to come close to the current English Premier League deal.

Outside English League action, the contract to televise domestic and European cup competitions has been split between ITV and the BSkyB/BBC consortium. ITV has the contract for the major European competition, the European Cup (Champions League), which has proven lucrative for Manchester United during the 1996/97 season. In its interim results, released in April 1997,

Manchester United said it expects to earn approximately £7.5m additional revenue for reaching the semi-finals of the competition, with television money being a major contributor. In addition to domestic viewing, the Premier League is popular viewing abroad, and the overseas rights for Premier League football are currently worth £8.5m per year, distributed equally to the Premier League clubs, minus administration and management costs at Premier League headquarters. The current contract is due for renewal at the end of the 1997/98 season and a substantial rise in value is expected.

PAY-PER-VIEW

However large the new television contracts are for both the English and Scottish Football League and the Premier League, the one over-riding force which has pushed the value of football clubs higher in recent times is the introduction of digital TV and the prospect of Pay-Per-View (PPV). The technology involved with the supply of digital television is beyond the scope of this book, but suffice to say, this new system of broadcasting could significantly change the entire leisure market. Digital television will allow improved home shopping, home banking, films on demand, and an enormous array of other services. One major change will be the introduction of PPV. The digital system will, in time, allow viewers the opportunity to choose which programmes they watch and when, and to be charged for them as they view. Sport is one area which should benefit.

The value of PPV to clubs will vary widely, with televised games involving the larger clubs, such as Newcastle, Manchester United, Chelsea, and Arsenal attracting the widest audiences. The smaller Premier League clubs such as Southampton and Wimbledon will find audiences harder to attract. BSkyB has already tested the PPV concept on a number of major boxing events, charging over 660,000 subscribers £10 each to watch English national hero Frank Bruno being taught a boxing lesson by Mike Tyson in March 1996. Since then they have charged for several other boxing events with similar success.

Rumours that BSkyB intended to test the PPV concept on Liverpool FC's European Cup-Winners Cup semi-final with Paris St Germain in April 1997 circulated, but failed to materialise. However, BSkyB is intent on introducing digital television in the Spring of 1998 and this makes the PPV concept much easier to market.

No one knows exactly what effect PPV will have on the football industry, the value of listed football companies, or on the current contracts for live football, but the Premier League has the option to review its BSkyB contract at the end of the 1998/99 season and this may signal the full introduction of PPV. The estimated value of PPV to the clubs varies a great deal between analysts and between different teams, but Nick Batram, an analyst at Greig Middleton, has conducted some detailed analysis on the subject. In his research he concluded that the Premier League "has a mandate to protect the interests of large and small clubs" which is reflected in the structure of the current TV deal. A small number of the big clubs, however, may feel aggrieved as they undoubtedly have greater appeal to the viewing public. Whether the current BSkyB deal will run in tandem with PPV is yet to be seen, but either way, BSkyB and the major football clubs are likely to benefit.

In his research, Batram placed each Premier League club into one of three categories, A to C, with the top clubs in A and the less attractive clubs in C. The February 1997 edition of *Sports Shares* newsletter adjusted these categories, but the findings were very similar.

Table 3.1: Pay-Per-View Categories (source: *Sports Shares*)

Category A

Manchester United*

Arsenal

Newcastle United*

Liverpool

Chelsea*

Aston Villa*

Tottenham Hotspur*

Category B

Sheffield Wednesday

Everton**

Leeds United*

Sunderland* (now relegated)

Middlesborough (now relegated)

Category C

Southampton*

West Ham**

Coventry City*

Leicester City**

Blackburn Rovers

Wimbledon

Derby County**

Nottingham Forest** (now relegated)

* Listed football clubs ** Expected to be listed during 1997/98

Batram's model concerned the pricing of each game and the potential revenue each club could generate from PPV each season. For games involving two category A teams, the charge would be £9; for games involving a category A team and a category B side the cost would be £6; and for games involving category A clubs versus category C teams the charge would be £3. Further research in the *Sports Shares* newsletter, based on Batram's findings, found that the potential earnings of category A teams were substantially higher than the current value of the BSkyB contract. This was shown using earnings estimates for Tottenham Hotspur as an example. The research used three scenarios – conservative, average and optimistic – to estimate the number of viewers for each category of game, each season, based on the estimated number of BSkyB subscribers able to receive digital broadcasts in the year 2000.

Table 3.2: Tottenham Hotspur, Potential Pay Per View Revenue (source: Greig Middleton, *Sports Shares*)

Tottenham Hotspur – Potential Pay Per View Earnings, Season 1999/2000

Game	Price	Matches	Conservative		Average		Optimistic	
			Audience	Revenue	Audience	Revenue	Audience	Revenue
A	£9	12	125,000	£13.5m	250,000	£27m	325,000	£35.1m
B	£6	10	75,000	£4.5m	150,000	£9m	200,000	£12m
C	£3	16	25,000	£1.2m	50,000	£2.4m	100,000	£4.8m
Total				£19.2m		£38.4m		£51.9m
45% revenue[1]				£8.64m		£17.29m		£23.36m

(1)   Revenue received by club is estimated to be divided between each participating team (45% each) and BSkyB (10%)

If, based on the conservative estimate for PPV, you add an additional £2.5m for other competitions and overseas rights, and assuming PPV replaces the current BSkyB contract, Tottenham could earn £11.1m in television revenue alone. This is a substantial increase to the sums the club could realistically earn now, and if the team were to progress in a European competition, a substantial amount could be added on top of this figure, driving the profitability and value of the club even higher.

Allowing for modest increases in gate receipts and other revenues, Tottenham's potential profit and loss account (excluding transfers) for the year ending 31 July, 2000 could be as shown in Table 3.3.

Table 3.3: Projected Profit & Loss account for Tottenham Hotspur, Year Ending 31 July, 2000. (source: *Sports Shares*)

Tottenham Hotspur – Year ending 31 July, 2000 (with 1997 estimates for comparison)

	31st July, 1997(E)	Conservative	Average	Optimistic
Turnover	£,000	£,000	£,000	£,000
Gate Receipts	13,500	14,500	14,500	14,500
Television[1]	4,800	11,140	19,780	25,855
Sponsorship	4,000	6,000	6,000	6,000
Conf. & Mkting	2,000	3,000	3,000	3,000
Merchandising	3,800	5,000	5,000	5,000
Total	28,100	39,640	48,280	54,355
Expenses	18,100	20,580	20,580	20,580
Operating Profit	10,000	19,060	27,700	33,775
Tax	3,000	5,718	8,310	10,133
Net Profit[2]	7,000	13,342	19,390	23,643

(1) Television estimates based on PPV revenue plus £2.5m for other competitions

(2) Excluding transfers

You can see the effect the introduction of PPV in the 1999/2000 season could have on the profit and loss account of Tottenham Hotspur, and you can imagine the impact this could have on the share price. The new television contract from BSkyB has already helped propel Tottenham's shares from 24p (adjusted for five-for-one share split in February 1997) at the end of the 1994/95 season to 107p at the end of the 1996/97 campaign. The introduction of PPV on the basis outlined above could lift them even higher.

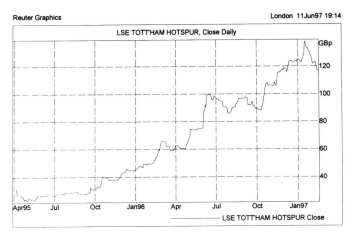

Figure 3.1: Tottenham Hotspur Share Price 1995-1997
(source: Reuters)

For a category C team, the picture is different. Research suggests the replacement of the BSkyB contract with the PPV example above could undermine the potential earnings of those clubs. For example, Southampton Football Club is situated in a small city with little support outside its home and surrounding towns. Over the past few seasons the club has narrowly escaped relegation to the First Division, and a game with a similar category side, such as Coventry, is unlikely to attract a large number of viewers. Games involving category C teams can only be priced at a low level, and using the same model as for Tottenham, Sports Shares estimates that Southampton could expect to receive just £1.283m per season from PPV on a conservative basis.

Table 3.4: Southampton Football Club, Potential Pay Per View Revenue (source: *Sports Shares*)							
Southampton Football Club – Potential Pay Per View Earnings, Season 1999/2000							
			Conservative		Average		Optimistic	
Game	Price	Matches	Audience	Revenue	Audience	Revenue	Audience	Revenue
A	£9	0	0	£0	0	£0	0	£0
B	£6	0	0	£0	0	£0	0	£0
C	£3	38	25,000	£2.85m	50,000	£5.7m	100,000	£11.4m
Total				£2.85m		£5.7m		£11.4m
45% revenue[1]				£1.283m		£2.565m		£5.13m

(1) Revenue received by club is estimated to be divided between each participating team (45% each) and BSkyB (10%)

Compared to the minimum a club in the Premier League can earn under the present contract, an estimated £5m, the introduction of PPV could be a disadvantage. As stated above, the Premier League has to take all its members' concerns into account when negotiating a new television deal and this would suggest a PPV contract would involve a mixture of the current deal and a new contract to cover the PPV element. Again, for clubs such as Tottenham, Manchester United and Chelsea, this may be frustrating and could cause some friction within the Premiership.

Table 3.5: Projected Profit & Loss account for Southampton Football Club, Year Ending 31st March, 2000. (source: *Sports Shares*)

Southampton Football Club – Year ending 31 March, 2000

	Conservative	Average	Optimistic
Turnover	£,000	£,000	£,000
Gate Receipts[1]	11,000	11,000	11,000
Television[2]	3,783	5,065	7,630
Commercial activity	9,000	9,000	9,000
Total	**23,783**	**25,065**	**27,630**
Expenses	18,000	18,000	18,000
Operating Profit	**5,783**	**7,065**	**9,630**
Tax	1,735	2,120	2,889
Net Profit[3]	**4,048**	**4,945**	**6,741**

(1) Assumes team has moved to new 25,000 all-seater stadium

(2) Television estimates based on PPV revenue plus £2.5m for other competitions

(3) Excluding transfers

The major risk for a club involved with the Premier League under PPV is a downgrade in its category. All football clubs go through lean periods, and slip from grace. Should Aston Villa, for example, fail to produce an attractive team which wins games, the club could face a downgrade from Category A to Category B. This would have a substantial effect on its television earnings which, in turn, may create financial problems at the club. This may force the manager to sell players to reduce his wage bill, which could create a drop in form. The risk is that a club may enter a vicious circle.

The opposite is also true. Should Southampton develop a number of youth players, or make some shrewd signings which improve the club's fortunes in the Premier League, and in the size of audience, the club could receive an upgrade to Category B. This could significantly boost the value of the company's television revenue, which may help the club attract better players – or hold on to the ones they have. This could improve their form still further, improving gate receipts and audience figures. The success of a club seems to be highly geared, firstly to playing Premier League football, and secondly to achieving the highest PPV category as possible.

OTHER SPORTS ON TELEVISION

The advent of satellite television in the UK has proven to be lucrative not only for football clubs, but for other popular sports which in the past had not received the coverage, or the financing, they required to expand.

The long-delayed introduction of professionalism in Rugby Union means that players can now be openly paid and the game can now be developed way beyond its previous amateur level. This new commercial era also brings with it a transfer market and an influx of foreign stars which has increased the marketability of the sport beyond *Rugby Special*, a highlights programme on BBC2 on a Sunday evening, and coverage of internationals from Twickenham. BSkyB has recognised this and purchased the exclusive rights to broadcast live England internationals to 2002 and English domestic rugby to 2001 in a deal worth £87.5m. BSkyB has also secured the exclusive rights to the Rugby Union European club competition which proved such a success during the 1996/97 season. The company set to benefit most from this deal is quoted sports company, Loftus Road. Not only does the club receive television revenue from BSkyB for its Queen's Park Rangers Football Club, from both the Football League contract and the parachute payments from the Premier League contract for seasons 1996/97 and 1997/98, but it will now also benefit from owning the 1996/97 Rugby Union Division One Champions, Wasps.

Over the past few years the ITV network has missed out on a great deal of the sporting events which have helped BSkyB and the BBC keep viewing levels up. In an attempt to redress the balance, ITV has stolen one traditional domain of the BBC, Formula One motor racing. This deal emphasises the increased competition for broadcast rights of major sporting events in the UK and internationally. The fact that the sport of motor racing, which depends so heavily on sponsorship, has remained on terrestrial television may prove to be a hurdle the satellite and cable channels find difficult to conquer. One of the key points which helped BSkyB secure the rights to Premier League football may, in turn, prove to be the company's downfall when negotiating for other key sporting events. The smaller number of viewers the satellite broadcaster attracts helped convince the Premier League it would not affect crowds at the games. Other major sporting events, such as motor racing and the Olympic Games, rely heavily on sponsorship to stage the events or fund the teams – and the sponsors demand exposure. To satisfy them, the event organisers have reportedly accepted smaller bids from terrestrial channels to keep the level of audiences higher. This is a problem which may stop BSkyB and other satellite/cable broadcasters from obtaining the rights to major international competitions.

OTHER BROADCASTING MEDIA

Away from television, some sports companies – particularly football clubs – have begun to investigate, and in some cases implement, alternative methods of broadcasting their games and producing additional revenue. Chelsea Village has commissioned production company Planet 24 to provide a radio station which is permitted to broadcast up to 28 times per year to an audience up to three miles from Chelsea's Stamford Bridge stadium. The broadcasts will include competitions, music and general news relating to the team and will also provide coverage of the game. The station is a commercial one and should attract advertising. The most interesting aspect of what is clearly a modest enterprise is that it could prove a dry run for clubs to run their own television channels in time.

Both Manchester United and Caspian, the leisure and media group which owns Leeds United, have plans to develop their own television channels. The channels are likely to be carried on local or even national cable networks and may operate on a PPV basis. Although they will not be able to broadcast live games, which are the sole property of BSkyB, the networks can show friendly, youth and reserve games. The channels are also likely to have access to any exclusive news from the club and may even prove to be a major channel for the sale of club merchandise.

Caspian seems very keen to exploit the national and international strength of its brand. Most teams in any major sport already have an official internet site, and a large proportion of 'hits' to these sites are from overseas. Caspian chairman Chris Akers has plans to broadcast live games on the internet. At present the technology is not quite ready, but in the near future subscribers may be able to pay to watch or listen to their favourite team play on their personal computer screen. With companies developing an increasing range of broadcast media, accessing live sport action is to become increasingly easy, and increasingly lucrative for the companies themselves.

CONCLUSION

The importance of BSkyB in the recent development of sport, financially, cannot be overstated. The company's policy of securing the rights to the major sporting events to boost subscription levels has created competition in the television market for these events which has, in turn, enormously increased the value of the contracts to broadcast them. This has injected a great deal of money into football, rugby and other, smaller sports, and transformed many of them.

The next stage of development is the impending introduction of digital television and PPV. This should not only increase demand for the rights to broadcast live games when the contracts come up for renewal, but for the larger sports clubs PPV could significantly increase the revenue they receive from television. The knack is to choose which listed sports clubs will benefit from the developments in the industry, and particularly those for which the information has not been reflected in the share price.

4

CHAPTER FOUR – OTHER SPORTS COMPANIES

Like the balls on a snooker table, sports companies are scattered around. They come in various shades, some are more valuable, and some are more visible than others. At the time of writing there are around 75 London Stock Exchange listed companies which may be classified in some way as a sports share. These are listed in Appendix 2, and some are covered in more detail in this chapter.

RETAILING

Sports retailing has been a tremendous growth sector. Look around the shops in your local high street and you will see that it is a competitive field, but a successful one. Key to its expansion has been the advertising-led boom in fashionable branded sportswear from such makers as Nike, Adidas and Reebok (see Chapter 7) which has transformed a fairly moribund industry into a fast-growth one. On the back of massive promotional budgets and huge sponsorship deals, branded sportswear has become a premier fashion item for young people. It has even become a fashion item for very young people indeed. According to research group Verdict, traditional childrens wear has been hit by "a burgeoning brand consciousness among the kids which has diverted significant chunks of spending . . . into the grateful cash registers of chains like JJB Sports and JD Sports".

A graphic illustration of the change is provided by Blacks Leisure Group, a hugely successful sportswear retailer which topped the league table for its share price performance in 1996. From 49.5p at the start of the year it boomed to finish the year at 386.5p – a rise of 681%. Yet in the previous four years the shares had halved and the company had struggled. So what changed? Back in 1992/93, trading conditions were tough not only for Blacks, but for other sports retailers as well. As the chairman said in his 1993 AGM statement, "1992 was a year which most sports retailers will be glad to have seen the back of, characterised, as it was, by fierce competition in the high street and lower overall levels of turnover. Many competitors slashed prices to attract customers with a view to reducing stock levels and generating cash flow." Blacks was forced to cut costs, sell off its unprofitable operations, and swallow a loss.

Since that time, a transformation has occurred both in the sports retailing market generally, and in Blacks Leisure in particular. According to the company's annual report and accounts for 1996, it made the following sales through its 92 stores in its latest financial year: 26,000 footballs, 46,000 swimsuits, and no fewer than 133,000 rucksacks. It went on to produce improvements in its interim results which the majority of companies can only dream of. Turnover during the period rose 36% to £42.2m which resulted in a pre-tax profit rise of 430% to £3.9m. Blacks recorded increased sales and improved margins in all three of its retail formats – First Sport, Blacks Outdoor and ActiveVenture. Blacks' stockbrokers have predicted pre-tax profits of £8.5m for 1997 and £11m for 1998.

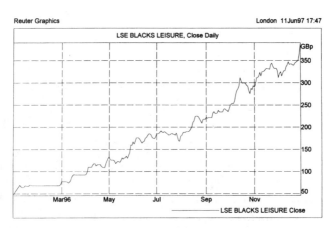

Figure 4.1: Blacks Leisure share price 1996 (source: Reuters)

John David Sports, founded by John Wardle and David Makin back in 1981, came to the market in late 1996 through a placing sponsored by BZW. Thirty per cent of the equity was placed on a high Price/Earnings multiple of 27.7 times which bore testimony to investors' enthusiasm for the sector. Furthermore, the shares began trading at a modest premium.

Trading principally under the name of JD Sports, the company has 72 nationwide outlets which stock fashionable branded sports and leisure wear by market leaders such as Adidas, Nike, Reebok, Ellesse, Fila, Kickers, and Umbro. This £2.1bn branded sportswear market, as distinct from general sports equipment, is undoubtedly a fast-growth sector, backed by heavy advertising by the brands, a helpful fashion trend, and a widespread increase in health consciousness. This is why JD was able to report a 60% leap in pre-tax profits to £6.7m on turnover of £56.4m for 1995/96. Looking to the future, growth is expected to come from two sources. Organic growth is anticipated from a continuation of existing trends, namely further growth in the leisure market, greater brand awareness, and some degree of consolidation within what is still a fragmented sector. Second, the company has plans to open up to 25 new stores per year, and can envisage potential for up to 200 stores in the UK, so it is not lacking in ambition.

One of JD's main competitors is the market leader JJB Sports. JJB was founded by former Blackburn Rovers professional footballer David Whelan, who bought his first store in Wigan. The expansion since then has been extraordinary and the company now operates over 160 stores, which produced a 58% rise in pre-tax profits to £20.3m in 1996. JJB plans to grow to over 200 stores in 1997, with more large superstores, and analysts are already pencilling in another 20% rise in profits. The company came to the stockmarket in November 1994, and has been another great success story. JJB shares have risen more than six-fold from their opening price of 77p (adjusted for share splits), and continue to sprint ahead.

What happens when this expansion of JJB Sports, JD Sports, and Blacks Leisure's 'First Sport' chain finally hits a wall will be interesting. Growth has been fuelled by the brand strength in 'fashion' sportswear which is not likely to continue indefinitely, and at some point the demand will slacken. Shareholders buying into these successful companies at prices which are supported by fancy prospective price-earnings ratios for 1998 of 28.2 times (JJB), 20.0 times (JD) and 18.6 times (Blacks) should take a moment to re-read the latter's 1992 statement. Success, but at what price?

SPORTSWEAR

As mentioned, the principal manufacturers who have forced the sportswear industry to break into a sweat have been overseas companies, led by Nike (US). There are some domestic producers though, one of the most dynamic of which is Hay & Robertson. This company has been through several guises over the years, having started life as a Scottish cloth manufacturer. By 1995 Hay had slipped into something more comfortable when it came to the stockmarket as a designer and manufacturer of women's evening wear, sold under the 'La Regina' label. At that point the company mentioned that it was seeking to acquire licences to produce and market leisurewear, which its new management, led by Lance Yates, has done with gusto.

A licence was acquired for 'Kangol' hats, and Hay followed this with 'Admiral' soccer kits and 'Cotton Oxford' rugby clothing brands. More recently the company concluded a deal with Dunlop for an exclusive sports and leisure clothing licence, and in late 1996 Hay reached agreement with Chelsea football club manager Ruud Gullit to produce a 'Ruud' line of clothing. The company is similarly developing an 'El Tel' brand with Terry Venables, the former England soccer manager. For what it's worth, the company has also secured the rights from the Football Association to produce England branded underwear, using the FA crest. Put these together with the more established brands of Kangol, Cotton Oxford, Admiral, Dunlop, and shirt agreements with seventeen major football clubs, and the company has a lot of attractive products to sell. The shares have already increased more than five-fold since September 1995, and Mr Yates is hoping to put Admiral at the helm of the fleet of British sportswear brands.

Pentland Group is a much larger company, capitalised at over £400m, and best known for its astonishing investment in Reebok USA in the 1980s. The company bought a 55.5% stake for just £50,000 in 1981 and cashed it in over the next ten years for enormous sums. The last 13% was sold in December 1991 for US$310m. Armed with this huge cash pile – the company said in 1992 "with net cash of £347m, we are seeing appropriate acquisitions" – Pentland was on the verge of buying Adidas from Bernard Tapie when the deal surprisingly fell through. Instead the company has invested in a range of sports labels including Ellesse, Kickers, and Speedo which have not really paid off. Pre-tax profits were virtually unchanged between 1994 and 1996, and the shares have failed to make any headway.

Robert H Lowe was in financial trouble a few years ago and lost £11.88m in 1993, but has recovered, due in part to the expansion of its sportswear division. For Euro '96 it manufactured the kit for Germany, Spain and Russia, but had a strip in every match since it also made the referees' and linesmens' kit. It has four factories operational and aims to raise its international profile. The company wants to expand into rugby league, basketball, and athletics strip to tide it over until World Cup fever strikes in 1998. Robert H Lowe is not, however, a pure play on the fashion for replica sports kit since it also comprises a packaging division.

Other companies in the sector include Claremont Garments, which makes football shirts for Marks & Spencer; Hawtin, which makes wetsuits amongst a range of other sporting products; Hi-Tec, which makes sports footwear; and H Young Holdings which manufactures under the 'Head' brand name.

FITNESS CLUBS

Drinks giant Whitbread owns David Lloyd Leisure, which is one of the
best known (and more expensive) chains of sports clubs which have
sprung up in recent years. Most of the industry is fragmented, with
small companies operating in small geographical areas, and with little
brand recognition. Indeed research company Mintel reports that the
largest ten operators have 273 clubs, or only 15% of the total clubs
estimated to be in operation. This seems likely to change, particularly
as some of the new listed companies begin ambitious expansion
programmes.

Fitness First was, as the name suggests, the forerunner in this sub-
sector, and it has set a trend for others to aspire to. The shares leapt
from 90.5p to 174.5p in their first six months of trading, with plenty
of clients responding to the call "making life better with affordable
fitness". Having started with one club in Bournemouth in 1992, the
company came to the market with six fitness centres, each built
around a well-equipped gymnasium and aerobics studio. More
expensive facilities such as swimming pools and racquet courts are not
offered, as the key is keeping the clubs affordable. To date the plans
seem to be soundly reasoned and successful.

Lady In Leisure followed the path to the market in 1997 as the first
chain of all-female fitness clubs. The company runs eight clubs at
present and is seeking to double in size. The shares were issued at 110p
and set a 13% premium on their first day of dealing, which is a far
from leisurely start. The clubs hope to prosper partly by removing the
pressure which overweight, older, or inexperienced gym users can feel
in a mixed-sex environment. By removing the intimidation the
company hopes to broaden the appeal of clubs for women.

Some similar sentiments have been expressed by Human Solutions
Group, a company which was launched on the OFEX in 1997. The
public face of the company is Sally Gunnell, the Olympic 400m
hurdling gold medallist. She says: "Our aim is to appeal to the 8 out of
10 women and 70% of men who do not exercise, by offering what we

like to call a 'no posers policy' together with state of the art facilities. Mainly in city/town centres and at an affordable price, we are removing barriers that have been in force for too long." Ms Gunnell has clearly moved on in her career, from jumping over barriers to moving them, and her basic premise is simple enough – that more and more people will respond to encouragement and take some steps to ensure a basic level of fitness. It remains to be seen whether the market will really expand, or whether the sector will consolidate into a handful of large chains, but there is no doubt that the health club sector is in an exciting development phase at present.

Vardon is a diversified leisure company with interests in bingo, holidays, and health and fitness clubs, but there is no question which is the growing element of the business. The company bought its health and fitness subsidiary, Archer, for £48.5m in 1996, and according to stockbrokers Teather and Greenwood, this "considerably enhanced the longer-term outlook for the entire group". Of course one benefit to any business is that membership fees are generally paid in advance, helping cash flow, and the stockbrokers also point out that a company with experience of running and refurbishing private clubs can also gain lucrative contracts in the public sector.

GOLF

Clubhaus was born in February 1996 following its demerger from the property company The Ex-Lands plc. The company operates two golf courses in Germany, one in France and is now running seven in the UK. It has been expanding rapidly and would seem to be on target to achieve its objective of having between 12 and 15 courses in the UK. The company aims to take advantage of what it sees as a depressed market, in terms of pricing, for golf courses in the UK, and of a shortage of quality courses in Europe. This strategy seems to be working with the shares climbing in value. The company has also acquired the Fox Club, an exclusive private members' club in central London. The company's strategy is to cross-market between its interests in golf and hospitality. It sees the private club as a benefit when it introduces its Clubhaus members' card expected in summer 1997.

PGA European Tour Courses is another company which owns and operates golf courses, as its name suggests. The company estimates that the European golf industry generates around £7bn per annum in revenue, with between 5m and 6m golfers playing on around 4,500 courses. Some 60% of these courses are in the UK, which is where the company has five of its eight courses. It aims to expand to twenty courses by the year 2000, on which 1m rounds of golf will be played.

MOTOR SPORTS

Given that Britain is probably the most important development centre for top-level motor racing outside of the United States, it is perhaps surprising how few investment opportunities there are. Many sizeable companies are privately owned, run by enthusiasts, and not open for investment. There are, however, two opportunities to get involved which could rev up your portfolio.

Bernie Ecclestone, the founder of the Formula One Constructors' Association, has decided to float the business on the New York and London stockmarkets. Salomon Brothers have apparently been appointed as advisers to the flotation which could value the business at up to £2bn. The estimated valuation is based on the potential for Pay-Per-View digital television and the income stream from media coverage. More than 130 countries, providing average audiences of 450m, receive transmissions of the annual seventeen race competition each year, making it the third most-watched TV sport after the Olympics and the soccer World Cup. With no heir apparent to his empire, Mr Ecclestone is likely to want to expand ownership of the business he has built up over the past 25 years, and he says that he wishes to protect his wife, who actually owns 80% of the business. She is set to become the richest woman in Britain after the flotation.

Brands Hatch Leisure, owners of the Brands Hatch, Oulton Park, Snetterton and Cadwell Park racing circuits is already listed. Although the company is best known for the hosting of motor racing events, which it can trace back to 1926, Brands Hatch also produces revenue through its Nigel Mansell Racing School, corporate entertainment, promotional facilities and the provision of the tracks for vehicle testing. There has been talk about using the circuits as venues for pop concerts, which seems appropriate in view of the youth of the company. Not only is Brands Hatch a relative newcomer to the market, but chief executive Nicola Foulston is the youngest of any public listed company. She is the 29-year old daughter of the late John Foulston, founder of Atlantic Computers. Nicola took charge at age 19, following his death in 1987, and has displayed a mix of tenacity and guile which has earned her respect and the title of Veuve Cliquot business woman of the year in 1997. The major shareholder with a 49.9% stake is Apax, the venture capital firm. Apax provided working capital for the company following a buyout which allowed Brands Hatch to purchase the freeholds which has opened the way for Nicola Foulston's expansion plans.

HORSE RACING

Horse racing is not especially well represented in the public company arena. The British Bloodstock Agency is probably the most important runner in the field, even though it is only capitalised at £3.8m. The company is an agent for buying and selling bloodstock, stallion shares and nominations; it also manages syndicates, and arranges shipping and insurance. A detailed explanation of the company's services with up-to-date news is available on the internet at http://www.bba.co.uk. British Bloodstock seems to be a well regarded company which has carved out a niche for itself and which has proved profitable. The shares have certainly run well for investors, rising from 40p at the start of 1992 to 90p five years later. That said, the performance has not been consistent, and the company is always likely to be reliant on outside factors such as bloodstock prices to keep up profits.

Newbury Racecourse plc is exactly that. The company owns and runs the racecourse, and also has an 18-hole golf course which generates a small amount of revenue. With only 1,900 shares in issue (at £4,000 each) the company is capitalised at £7.6m and has its shares traded on a matched-bargain basis on OFEX. Whilst all kinds of things could change, Newbury Racecourse gives the impression of being a well run but rather gentlemanly company which is probably for enthusiasts only. Newbury may be a thoroughbred, but probably not a galloping investment. Details of races, facilities and bookings are available on the internet web site at http://www.raceweb.com/newbury. Chepstow Racecourse, another public company, is a smaller cousin to Newbury, and Lingfield Park racecourse is part of Arena Leisure, having been purchased for £10m in 1997. Lingfield Park can boast one of just three all-weather tracks in the UK which virtually guarantees racing in the harsh winter months, and with the management also having contracts to run the racing at Brighton, Folkestone, Fontwell, and Plumpton, they control around 12% of the UK fixture list annually. Like Newbury, Lingfield Park has an 18-hole golf course adjacent to the race courses.

BETTING

Should you go to the races at Newbury, Chepstow, or Lingfield Park, horse racing's principal contribution to the stockmarket will be staring you in the face. Or in the wallet. Betting is for most racegoers an integral part of the occasion, and there are some large companies competing for punters' money. Ladbroke Group is the £2.7bn colossus of the sector, although this includes the Hilton International hotel chain which makes twice as much profit as the betting and gaming division. The latter is no slouch though, bringing in £84.9m in profits in 1996. This was a considerable improvement over 1995, which was made a difficult year by the introduction of the National

Lottery. Ladbroke has responded by cutting costs and undertaking new marketing initiatives for new products. Football betting increased because of the Euro '96 tournament, and the average bet crept over £5 for the first time. One painful interlude was the extraordinary string of seven winners at one race meeting by jockey Frankie Dettori which cost the company £8m. Stanley Leisure betting shops lost £2m, and the overall cost to the industry of Mr Dettori's extraordinary feat in September 1996 is estimated at £18m.

William Hill is a major bookmaker, with around 1,700 betting shops, which turned in some £50.3m in profits in 1996. It is rumoured to be worth around £500m, yet you will not find it listed under its own name. This is because it is part of the Brent Walker Group, which is capitalised at only £13m. How can this be? The answer lies with Brent Walker's huge £1.3bn debt burden which makes the company of dubious value in spite of its undoubted assets. It seems likely that William Hill will be sold in the near future, possibly to brewing firm Bass, which already owns 930 UK betting shops through its Coral chain.

Zetters Group, the pools operator, has struggled to overcome the impact of the National Lottery, which has diverted customers' discretionary funds, and this is one sector which has not benefited from the football boom. The government has not been entirely insensitive to the needs of the industry though, and has slackened some of the stringent regulations to a modest degree. In June 1996 legislation changed to allow the installation of up to two fruit machines in each betting shop, with a maximum cash payout of £10. This may not sound like a major change, but Stanley Leisure expects these to add £1.5m to its profits in the first year of introduction. Another addition is the '49's' game, which is a daily numbers draw clearly designed to compete with the Lottery.

PERIPHERAL BUSINESSES

There is a whole range of other businesses which can be classified as sports shares, depending on how far the definition is stretched. Take insurance, for example. Footballers are highly-paid, highly expensive assets for clubs in these days of spiralling costs, and as with all fragile assets, they need to be insured. Alan Shearer, Newcastle's record signing for £15m, is insured through specialist sports broker Windsor which is the clear leader in this market. It is already the "world's leading specialist" in sports and personal accident insurance, according to the company's broker. Commercial, leisure and sports insurance accounts for 52% of total turnover, so it qualifies as being the company's core business. In September 1995 Windsor acquired motor racing insurance broker RCM, and it sees particular scope for expansion on the track, as well as in the field of rugby.

Football is nevertheless the most important sport, accounting for 60% of the company's sports revenues. Some 23 account handlers work on football alone, and they are at their busiest in August and September as the season starts and many transfers take place. With football stars earning far greater sums now, and clubs being forced to pay higher and higher transfer fees, premiums must rise accordingly as more cover is needed.

IMS is another premium service provider, this time providing information. The company is the product of a management buyout from bookmaker William Hill in 1992, and provides telephone information services ranging from horse racing to Newcastle United's TEAMtalk phone-in service. Chairman and managing director Bill Wilson claims IMS handles 50 million calls a year on its premium rate telephone lines. The company has invested heavily in interactive technology for the collection of information and operates lines for newspapers, magazines and even voice mail services for corporate clients. The company appears to be a good cash generator as marginal costs are very low. Profits for 1996 rose from £2.71m to £3.26m on turnover of £12.4m (£10.3m).

GlycoSport, which is traded on OFEX (see Chapter 6), produces a 'natural energy drink' which has been developed in the USA from a medical formula for diabetics. The drink does not contain sugar or other forms of glucose, but apparently "releases energy naturally, prior to and during demanding activity". GlycoSport is endorsed by former women's 400m hurdles world record holder Sally Gunnell MBE. "I first started using the original Glycophos formula in 1993 and have been using GlycoSport as a structured part of my training programmes," she says. The finished product is already on sale in Boots across the country, and in various other stores in the North West. The European soft drink market is worth £600m per year, with energy drinks accounting for £300m. The market place is a large one, but it appears GlycoSport owns just the UK license and this restricts the potential sales dramatically.

CCI is an intriguing little company which is the undisputed market leader for the manufacture of clay pigeons in the UK. The company has a new factory in Corby which allows sufficient capacity for the company to seek export opportunities, and the directors have certainly done a good job to date. Earnings per share rose 44% in 1996, and the shares exhibited a wonderfully consistent upward trend in their first eighteen months of stock exchange listing. There are incentives for the directors, who will achieve full conversion of their founder shares into ordinary shares if the share price reaches 275p by May 2000.

There is a wide range of other sports companies which could also have been covered in this section, and if you wish to cast your net more widely, you can do your own homework without too much difficulty. The names and addresses of other sports share companies are listed in Appendix 2, and you can write for their annual report and accounts. These useful documents will give you a great deal of information on the companies, and are available free of charge. Most companies are extremely obliging, regarding their annual report as an important marketing tool, and will send a copy promptly on request.

5

CHAPTER FIVE – HOW TO SELECT SPORTS SHARES

Now you know all about sports companies in the UK, how can you profit from them? The simple answer is by buying the shares of those most likely to benefit from the increased enthusiasm for the sector and the leisure activities they encompass. But which shares are those?

This chapter examines some of the key points to look out for when selecting the sports shares which are most likely to perform well. Although this is not a comprehensive guide to selecting shares, it is a guide to the specific areas of stock selection which may be most applicable. One point to be aware of, however, is that no adviser can possibly give you a foolproof method of selection. There are no easy answers, because if there were, all investors would always buy the right shares, markets would be priced perfectly, and there would never be any anomalies for you to profit by. Share analysis is an art, not a science, and each company must always be judged on its individual merits. That said, it can help to have a framework for your analysis, and the points covered in this chapter should help.

THE INDUSTRY

When evaluating the potential of a sports company it is important to research the entire industry in which it operates. This may seem like common sense, but is surprisingly overlooked by many. It is important to evaluate the size of the market, the number of competitors in the market and your potential investment's standing within the industry.

The sportswear retailers covered in Chapter 4 provide a good example. All three have performed extremely well and this has been reflected in some very impressive share price movements. However, the May 1997 edition of *Sports Shares* cast doubt on the potential for future growth in the industry, citing future over-capacity as a potential problem for the companies involved. It seems likely the market will become saturated and levels of earnings growth will probably slip in the future, and this is likely to rein in the shares' performance.

To help determine the size and potential of a market, a good start is the company's annual report. Although this is likely to paint a rosy picture, it can provide some insight to the company's operations. Other good sources include trade magazines and industry surveys. These are often produced by independent marketing groups, universities, stockbrokers or even accountants. For example, "Women Keeping Fit", a New Leisure Markets report in 1996, predicted that the £423m spent by women on fitness-related activity in 1995 will rise to £750m by the year 2000. *Sports Shares* newsletter brought this to the attention of its readers when Lady in Leisure plc, the company which operates women-only health clubs, placed £1.7m of its shares on the AIM at 110p. The shares rose to 130.5p within days of listing.

COMPARATIVE COMPANIES

An obvious technique for considering the value of a company is to compare it with other similar companies in the same sector. Sometimes there are no close competitors, but where there are, it is possible to use various ratings such as Price/Earnings ratios which allow you to compare like with like. Again, the sports retailers, John David Sports, JJB Sports, and Blacks Leisure, provide a neat example, and more of the companies operating in the various sports sectors are detailed in Chapter 4.

BRAND IMAGE

The brand of a company or its product, particularly in the sports industry, can have a substantial effect on the selling power and sustainability of a company's earnings. A company's brand image may be just a local one like Preston North End, a national one like Newcastle United, or an international one like Manchester United. Whichever it may be, it often has the potential to be exploited further, but it is the quality which will determine how far and for how long. In a research document issued by Nick Batram of Greig Middleton, he suggested that the Newcastle United brand had not reached the "core or depth of support nationally or internationally that some of the other large clubs have". The report continued: "If Newcastle had a bad season we would expect their sales of branded products to fall at a proportionately greater rate than say Manchester United's sales if they had a poor run on the pitch." Therefore, when choosing a sports company which relies greatly on its brand, make sure it is a strong one, and if it is not, be prepared to take on additional risk when assuming it will become a sustainable brand.

MANAGEMENT

The quality or experience of the company's management can have a large bearing on the rating it receives in the market – and the rating you should place on it. The best place to examine a company's management is its annual report which often provides a profile of each board member. Use your own judgement to determine whether you feel they are up to the job in hand. One of the other key areas to examine is incentives. Are the directors adequately motivated to see the company succeed? Incentives can come in many different forms. They include options to buy shares at specific prices in the future. The more difficult it is for the directors to qualify for them, the better (within reason). Many companies simply use options as another form of payment, but those which require a certain level of earnings per share, or a particular level of share price performance before they become exercisable, are among the best types.

Caspian Group's directors each have options to subscribe for shares at 13p, a significant discount to the share price. But to qualify for them the shares must first, for three consecutive years, increase in market value such that they are in the top third as measured by the FTSE Small Companies Index (excluding investment trusts). This means the company has to outperform the majority of its peers for three consecutive years, providing a strong incentive for the board to make sure the company performs well.

Shareholdings are also a good incentive to perform well. If the directors have invested a large amount of their own money into the company's shares, this provides a strong motivation to build the value of those holdings by improving the profitability of the business. They are also showing other investors that they are confident in the future of the business. In fact, many investors place a great deal of faith in directors' dealings. They use reported purchases as a trigger to invest themselves, and directors' selling in a similar way.

In January 1997, *Sports Shares* newsletter reported that JJB Sports director Andrew Thomas had bought 3,000 shares in JJB at 295p on 10th December 1996, taking his holding to 12,000. The article went on to state that his timing appeared impeccable as JJB had just issued an upbeat trading statement. Five months later the shares had reached 500p – a rise of 70%.

PRODUCT JUDGEMENT

The key to successful analysis is often no more than common sense. Take a look at the underlying products and try to discern whether there is likely to be a continuing and growing market for them. Then decide whether the company is likely to make the most of its opportunities. Sometimes, of course, this second stage is not necessary.

Snakeboard, a company floated on the AIM in 1996, is a good example. Offered at 3p, the shares moved up in early trading to 3.75p, and finance director Tim Odell felt confident this would be just the start. He explained in an interview that the company sold over 100,000 of its boards, which are like pivoted skateboards, in 1995/96, and planned to use the £3m raised from the flotation to move into the lucrative US and Japanese markets. The company estimated the US market in 'extreme sports' goods to be worth over US$ 3bn per year, and to be growing at an annual rate up to 30%. Plans were also advanced for diversification into snowboards together with branded clothes, footwear, and protective gear – all of which seemed very sensible.

Unfortunately it was all too easy to have serious doubts. A company video titled 'Hellburger' described snakeboarders as "crazed lunatic psychopathic losers who have no regard for life, limb, or flesh", and it was tempting to wonder whether investors had to fit the same mould. The big question mark was over the sustainability of the firm's product, which could turn out to be just another teenage craze. Mr Odell pointed to the superiority of snakeboards over skateboards, which have been popular for around thirty years now, but in a sport said to "abandon risk management" this is not something to be advised for potential investors. The case was not proven, and when an innovative fashion-sensitive product is coupled with overseas expansion – a notoriously difficult strategy to undertake successfully – it is best to steer clear. In November 1996 the *Sports Shares* newsletter said: "We would be inclined to slither away for the moment."

Sure enough, Snakeboard issued not one but two profit warnings within six months of its flotation, which caused *The Times* to say that Snakeboard "has to be the worst AIM stock ever". The company found that sales dropped beneath expectations, failed to meet its illustrative projections framed only six months earlier, and the shares skidded down to just half their placing price.

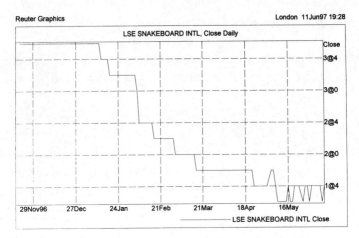

Figure 5.1: Snakeboard share price 1996-97 (source: Reuters)

In the case of sports clubs, and particularly football clubs, the success of the company depends to a great extent on the team and its performance on the field (or rink, court, pitch, track) of play. The dream of all supporters is to see their team play against the best teams and to win, and this should also be the desire of investors as success on the field often leads to success off it. The classic example is Manchester United. The team has won the Premiership title five times between 1991 and 1997, and in the 1996/97 season they reached the semi-finals of the coveted European Champions' League competition. During those years the club has listed on the stockmarket and, after a disappointing start, the shares have risen by an astounding 966% between the start of the 1992/93 season and the end of the 1996/97 campaign.

Another factor which can determine the financial viability of a sports club is its style of play. An attractive team, playing an attacking and flowing game is far more entertaining to watch than a boring, defensive style of play. Therefore, the more attractively a team plays, the more likely it is to attract additional viewers and supporters across the country and internationally. Newcastle United football club, for example, has a reputation for playing attacking football which produces goals (at both ends of the pitch). For this reason, a football fan is more likely to want to watch Newcastle play than, say, Leeds United which has a reputation for playing defensively. This factor can apply to attendances at the ground, to the potential PPV audience, and to which category they fall into (see Chapter 3). Personalities are also a key factor in attracting both audience figures and merchandise sales. The introduction of a domestic or foreign star to a club can stimulate supporters to renew their season ticket, or buy a new replica kit with the new star player's name on it. When Tottenham Hotspur signed German star Jurgen Klinsmann for one season, the sale of replica shirts with his number and name stencilled on the back rocketed, making a great deal of money for both the kit manufacturer (Pentland) and for Tottenham.

LOCAL KNOWLEDGE

In terms of sports clubs, plus some smaller local listed companies, a little local knowledge can go a long way. Local newspapers, television, radio, advertising and gossip can sometimes provide investors with unparalleled access to information about their local sports teams – information which the national media may cast aside due to a lack of space or interest. When conducting research on a local sports company, use the advantage you have in gaining access to local archive research.

LEAGUE POSITION

One key factor which can affect the performance of a sports team on the stockmarket is its performance on the field (see Product Judgement above). A good example of this is the performance of Southampton Leisure Holdings' and Sunderland's shares in the latter half of the 1996/97 football season. Sunderland came to the market with an apparently reasonable chance of survival in the Premier

League (14th place on 24 December 1996). Southampton were in a more precarious position, placed 19th on the 14th January. Both sets of shares had jumped to large premiums on their opening of trading, but as the season went on, and Sunderland's form on the field deteriorated, the share prices fell in line with the club's league position. By the end of March, Southampton's share price had reached its low point of 70p, less than half its peak price of 153.5p. This coincided with the club's drop to the bottom of the Premier League. From this point on the fortunes of the two clubs differed. The graph clearly shows the upturn in Southampton's share price as performances on the field improved, pushing the club up the table and clear from relegation by the time the season ended in early May. Over the same period Sunderland's poor run of form continued and the share price also continued to fall until 11th May when Sunderland were relegated. On the first day of trading after the team went down, Sunderland's shares fell an additional 8%.

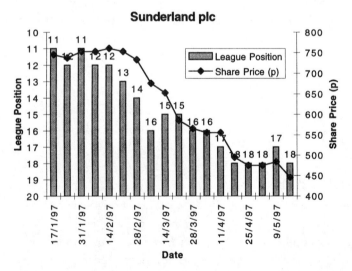

Figure 5.2: share price and league position for Sunderland FC (source: *Sports Shares*)

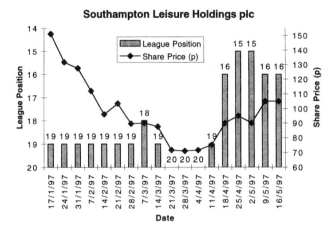

Figure 5.3: share price and league position for Southampton FC
(source: *Sports Shares*)

At the other end of the scale, Manchester United shares surprisingly
fell once the 1996/97 Premier League title had been wrapped up. The
news prompted investors to take profits and the ensuing sell-off saw
the shares slip from 661p to a low of 577.5p just seven days later.
Sometimes it is better to travel than to arrive.

For lower division clubs the chance of promotion is a factor which
can add value to the company's shares. In the 1995/96 football season
Preston North End won the Third Division championship and
obtained automatic promotion to the Second Division. The shares
had, since flotation in September 1994, remained at 400p, but in
March 1996 investors began to recognise the increased exposure and
revenue promotion to the Second Division might bring and over the
next six months the shares jumped 50% to 600p. For Sheffield
United, the story was all too different. The First Division side reached
the 1996/97 play-off final for promotion to the Premier League just
six months after the club was reversed into Conrad. United lost one-
nil to Crystal Palace and the shares dropped 34.6% the following day.

For Manchester United, the Premier League title was already factored into the price, but for Preston and Sheffield the news had a much greater effect on the share price.

MARKET SENTIMENT

The stockmarket is often viewed as an impersonal 'entity' – a place where prices are mysteriously changed and transactions automated. In fact it is an amalgamation of thousands of individuals, all with their own personalities, decision-making processes, concerns, hopes, ambitions, and fears. As such, it is subject to the vagaries of fashion and what is loosely called 'sentiment'. What this really means is that not all decisions are coolly rational, but that emotions sometimes come to the fore and investors can be swept along on a tide of rising or falling prices. Add in the likelihood of many investors having an emotional tie as supporters of a team, and sentiment can play an important part in the valuation of sports shares.

When trying to understand what implications this nebulous thing referred to as sentiment may have, investors must grasp the essential point that the market discounts events in advance, and that once something has happened it is generally too late to profit from it. This catches novice investors out time and time again. One potential investor, who happened to be a fan of Chelsea football club, telephoned when the team had just put together a string of good results and looked set to challenge at the very top of the Premiership. He was excited, things were going well, and he wanted to buy some shares. Unfortunately for him, the market had beaten him to it, and the price was already well ahead of events and had risen by more than a third over the previous month. At that point he would be well advised to sell, rather than to buy, precisely because other ill-informed investors were leaping into the market and paying more than the company was really worth. With football clubs in particular, it is a common observation that share prices 'overshoot' when sentiment-driven trade occurs. When results are good, the price goes too high, and vice versa. The lesson to learn is that it is sometimes better to buy when the team performance has been bad (it may improve) and to sell when things are going really well and the fans are all dreaming of glory.

The Chelsea example was covered in the February 1997 issue of the *Sports Shares* newsletter. Chelsea had just trounced Liverpool 4-2 in the FA Cup and moved up to fifth in the Premiership, causing the shares to rise to 166.5p, from just 124p a month before. The newsletter concluded that "we would be sellers at present" and the shares were back at 124p inside a month.

STOCKBROKERS RESEARCH

Another good information source is stockbrokers. Stockbrokers, in an attempt to stimulate business, produce research suggesting which stocks and shares their clients should consider buying and selling. By becoming a client, or even by simply requesting the information, a stockbroker can sometimes provide you with detailed research on the company in which you are interested. One word of caution though. Each listed company has an appointed broker and it is in their interests to be positive about a company which is one of their clients. Although this does not mean the brokers will not give best advice, some of their comments and forecasts may be a little optimistic. One other point: a company's broker is unlikely to place sell advice on the company and therefore a downgrade to a 'hold' should sometimes be taken as a 'sell'.

PRESS COMMENT

The press can also provide good information on companies. The majority of the national Sunday press provides recommendations and the weekly *Investors Chronicle* offers up to six tips in each edition. The drawback of following the press' recommendations is that thousands of other private investors also do so, and this often forces the tip's price up on the morning of publication. Also, it is important to understand that journalists are often acting on a tip or piece of information gleaned elsewhere and this information, or their judgement, can be as misguided as anyone else's. For example, in November 1996 the *Investors Chronicle* placed a sell note on the shares of sportswear company Pentland Group. The shares subsequently fell 3.5p to 90p on the Friday morning (the day of publication). In the following issue of *Sports Shares* the newsletter questioned the *Investors Chronicle*'s decision and shortly afterwards the shares hit 118p.

Sports Shares is the only newsletter devoted to this sector. It is a monthly publication offering independent advice and comment on the sector, and specific buy and sell recommendations on companies. A special subscription offer for readers is printed in the rear of this book. Should you require further details please call The McHattie Group of Bristol on 0117 925 8882.

INSTITUTIONAL HOLDINGS

It is often a useful sign to see whether other investors are buying or holding the shares in which you are interested, particularly when these investors are institutional. Pension funds, insurance companies, trusts, and a wide range of other 'institutions' invest in shares, and when they do so it is often an encouraging sign that the company has a stable future. Their managers are required to have high standards of analysis and prudence, and they are of course accountable for their performance. As a general rule, if a number of well-respected institutions have shareholdings, this is regarded as a good sign. An example is provided by European Leisure, a snooker and bars/discotheque company which suffered financial problems in the late 1980s with the result that the banks took control with a holding of more than two-thirds of the equity. It was a key sign of recovery when, in October 1996, the company was able to bring some institutions back into the company with a successful rights issue. Clive Bastin, the company's chairman, said that European Leisure would "benefit from a conventional capital structure and broad institutional ownership" and later added that this was "a watershed in our prospects going forward".

FORECASTS

One way of finding out what other analysts think of a stock is to obtain details of their earnings forecasts for the company in question. These can be obtained from stockbrokers' research, or press comment, but one of the easiest ways is to purchase the information which has already been compiled and clearly presented. One of the most recognised publications of this type of research is *The Estimate Directory* (TED), which is produced by Edinburgh Financial Publishing Limited. The book, produced monthly, provides a round-up of major broker's estimates for each individual company listed on the London Stock Exchange. Earnings forecasts can be wrong, but a consensus view may provide you with the reassurance you require to go ahead and make a purchase, or to stay away from a company you thought was a good prospect.

CRUNCHING NUMBERS

The topic of earnings estimates leads us nicely into the realm of company accounts. This is an area which can baffle many and cause some to avoid this important area of analysis completely. An in-depth breakdown of the way a company's accounts are constructed is beyond this book, but those wishing to further their knowledge of this important area of research can find many good books on the subject in any major bookshop. However, some of the useful tools and tricks which are appropriate to the sports sector are outlined below.

Earnings per share (EPS) is a figure easily gleaned from a company's accounts and is extremely useful when determining whether the shares are expensive or not. The use of forecasts and comparisons (see above) can also help determine the shares true value. The EPS figure basically represents the amount of company profits, after tax, which is attributable to each share. The history of this figure alone can be useful in determining the strength of a company's profit record. When divided into the share price, a figure is produced which can be compared with others in the same sector. The price/earnings (P/E) ratio is a figure which gives the number of years it would take for the company to produce enough earnings, at that level, to equal the current share price. The higher the figure, the longer it will take, and therefore, the more expensive is the share. The average P/E for the UK stockmarket (measured by the FTSE All Share Index) in May 1997 was 18.5 times, but for a more accurate picture it is important to compare the company's figure with either the sector in which it is classified (eg Leisure & Hotels), or the sub-sector to which it belongs (eg soccer clubs, or sportswear retailers). The closer you can get to the company's direct competitors, the better.

For those companies operating in fast growing markets with equally fast potential earnings growth, you can expect them to command a P/E ratio far higher than a large industrial company operating on low margins with slower earnings growth. JJB Sports, for example, was featured in the May 1997 edition of the *Sports Shares* newsletter as commanding a forecast P/E for 1998 of 27 times, based on earnings forecasts gleaned from *The Estimate Directory*. In contrast, leisure equipment manufacturer Hawtin had a forecast P/E for 1998 of just eight. Hawtin's shares were made a medium-term buy.

Football and other types of sports club are different to the majority of other companies. The major problem with valuing them is the presence of several unmeasurable and volatile elements. Many of these factors are outlined in this chapter and elsewhere in the book, including the presently unmeasurable potential of Pay-Per-View (PPV) television, transfer developments and future league performance. Many analysts have tried to simplify the process of attributing values based on many combinations of ratios and formulae, both simple and complex. The most basic is probably the Market Capitalisation/Turnover ratio. This formula simply involves the division of the market value of a company by its turnover, and the higher this is, the more expensive the shares. Table 5.1 shows the range of numbers which are thrown up by this calculation. The figures are intended to be used as a comparative tool for clubs, with Manchester United the model to which all football clubs aspire.

Table 5.1 Market Capitalisation/Turnover (MC/T) Ratio

Company/Team	Market Capitalisation*	Estimated Turnover**	MC/T Ratio
Chelsea Village	£161.25m	£20.4m	7.90
Manchester United	**£387.81m**	**£75m**	**5.17**
Newcastle United	£162.98m	£38m	4.29
Tottenham Hotspur	£101.12m	£28.1m	3.60
Caspian Group	£63.09m	£19.5m	3.24
Sunderland	£32.21m	£13.6m	2.37
Preston North End	£7.92m	£4.05m	1.96

*based on prices on 9 June, 1997

**forecasts for 1997 (source: Greig Middleton, Investment Research, 9 April, 1997)

From the simple to the extreme, we reintroduce the Pay-Per-View model from Chapter 3. The Nick Batram inspired PPV model generated the profit and loss (P&L) forecasts for Tottenham Hotspur for the year ending 31 July, 2000 as shown in Table 5.2. In producing this table, *Sports Shares* increased all the other forms of revenue production on a conservative basis and increased expenses significantly to reflect the potential for increases in players' wage demands. As you can see, the table has also been extended to include several additional pieces of essential information. The average number of shares in issue enables the all important earnings per share figure to be calculated by dividing the net profit by the number of shares.

For the year 2000 estimates, the earnings per share figure has been calculated using a discount factor of 15% per annum to bring them into line with today's figures. Again, this is a particularly conservative figure. To do this you must perform the following calculation:

$$\text{Net Present Value} = \frac{\text{EPS}}{(1+r)^y}$$

where   EPS = Earnings per Share
   r = rate of discount (i.e. 15% = 0.15)
   y = number of periods (ie years) to discount

For example, to adjust Tottenham's 'conservative' EPS figure of 13.33p the following calculation has been performed.

$$\text{Net Present Value} = \frac{13.33}{(1+0.15)^3}$$

$$\text{Net Present Value} = \frac{13.33}{(1.5209)}$$

$$\text{Net Present Value} = 8.76p$$

As the table shows, the 'conservative' EPS figure is reduced from 13.33p to 8.76p; the 'average' EPS figure falls from 19.37p to 12.73p; and the 'optimistic' EPS figure drops from 23.61p to 15.53p. To determine a useful value for the shares a representative P/E figure must be decided upon. In this case *Sports Shares* followed Nick Batram's example and used a P/E figure of 18, which is "in line with a number of quoted TV companies". By multiplying the EPS figure by the P/E factor of 18 a fair value for the shares can be calculated.

If Tottenham Hotspur meets *Sports Shares'* conservative estimate for revenue growth, then to discount this future performance the shares, at the time of writing, ought to be 158p. If Tottenham were to match the average estimate then the shares should be 229p, and if the optimistic forecast for profits was reached then 279p would be a fair value. All three estimates are well in excess of the Tottenham share price at the time of writing.

Table 5.2 Projected Profit & Loss account for Tottenham Hotspur, Year Ending 31 July, 2000. (source: *Sports Shares*)

Tottenham Hotspur – Year ending 31 July, 2000

	Conservative	Average	Optimistic
Turnover	£,000	£,000	£,000
Gate Receipts	14,500	14,500	14,500
Television[1]	11,140	19,780	25,855
Sponsorship	6,000	6,000	6,000
Conf. & Mkting	3,000	3,000	3,000
Merchandising	5,000	5,000	5,000
Total	39,640	48,280	54,355
Expenses	20,580	20,580	20,580
Operating Profit	19,060	27,700	33,775
Tax	5,718	8,310	10,133
Net Profit[2]	13,342	19,390	23,643
Avg. No. of Shares	100.119m	100.119m	100.119m
Earnings per Share	13.33p	19.37p	23.61p
Earnings per Share[3]	8.76p	12.73p	15.53p
Share Price[4]	158p	229p	279p

(1) Television estimates based on PPV revenue plus £2.5m for other competitions
(2) Excluding transfers
(3) Earnings per share based on annual net present value growth of 15% for three years to 31/7/00)
(4) Share price based on P/E of 18 – in line with many TV companies

The same exercise has been conducted for Southampton Leisure Holdings in Table 5.3. The key difference is that the P/E ratio has been reduced to 15 to reflect the perceived lower potential for earnings growth. The figures also allow for the club's planned move to a new 25,000 all-seater stadium for the 1999/2000 season and assume that the club maintains its Premier League status (a position which has been threatened in recent years). A loss of its position in the top flight, whilst not disastrous, would have a substantial negative affect on the share price.

Table 5.3: Projected Profit & Loss account for Southampton Leisure Holdings, Year Ending 31 March, 2000. (source: *Sports Shares*)

Southampton Leisure Holdings – Year ending 31 March, 2000

Turnover	Conservative £,000	Average £,000	Optimistic £,000
Gate Receipts[1]	11,000	11,000	11,000
Television[2]	3,783	5,065	7,630
Commercial activity	9,000	9,000	9,000
Total	**23,783**	**25,065**	**27,630**
Expenses	18,000	18,000	18,000
Operating Profit	**5,783**	**7,065**	**9,630**
Tax	1,735	2,120	2,889
Net Profit[3]	**4,048**	**4,945**	**6,741**
Avg. No. of Shares	26.9m	26.9m	26.9m
Earnings per Share	15.03p	18.37p	25.04p
Earnings per Share[4]	9.89p	12.08p	16.46p
Share Price[5]	**148p**	**181p**	**247p**

(1) Assumes team has moved to new 25,000 all-seater stadium
(2) Television estimates based on PPV revenue plus £2.5m for other competitions
(3) Excluding transfers
(4) Earnings per share based on annual net present value growth of 15% for three
     years to 31/7/00)
(5) Share price based on P/E of 15 (lower due to perception of lower earnings growth
     potential)0

Again, all other revenue streams have been increased on a conservative basis and expenses have risen to reflect increasing wage demands from players. Having determined the three EPS estimates the calculation has been performed to find the net present value of those estimated future earnings. By multiplying the adjusted EPS figure by the reduced P/E of 15 we find that on a conservative basis the shares are valued at 148p. Using the average figure the shares are valued at 181p and using the optimistic valuation the shares are valued at 247p – a 135% premium to the company's share price at the end of the 1996/97 season.

TAKEOVER SPECULATION

Even badly run companies with inconsistent profit records can produce great returns for investors – if you can buy before a takeover. When bidding to take over a rival company, predators normally have to persuade shareholders to sell by offering a price well in excess of the prevailing market price, sometimes yielding excellent profits. This is why rumours of a takeover can drive share prices dramatically higher, and why hosts of investors spend time trying to find the next takeover target. Bids happen in all sectors, including sports, and there are some superb examples.

Over the space of two days in October 1996 the value of Manchester United shares jumped 23.5% as rumours of a possible takeover bid coincided with the emergence of details of a 480p per share bid from VCI plc which had been rejected earlier that year. The rumours surrounded three potential bidders. These were Granada, Whitbread and US marketing company IMG. All three denied an interest in the club, although three months later Granada chairman Gerry Robinson admitted that he had been urged to buy into the club in the early 1990s and that it was now "too late".

Once an unfounded bid rumour recedes the share price of the rumoured target can slip back, but have heart – the rumour is now 'out there'. Once a company comes into play, the rumour almost never goes away. This can place support below a company's share price, offering some downside protection. If, after a period of time, the company's share price falls back the rumour mill is often quickly restarted, helping to push the share price back upwards again. The extent of the support can vary greatly, but it is almost always there to some degree.

Recently a different form of takeover has become popular in the sports industry – the reverse takeover. During the 1996/97 season three soccer clubs came to the stockmarket using this route, as outlined in Chapter 2. The three examples are Secure Retirement's acquisition of Southampton Football Club (renamed Southampton Leisure Holdings plc), Conrad's purchase of Sheffield United (renamed Sheffield United plc) and Mosaic's acquisition of Bolton Wanderers (renamed Burnden Leisure plc).

The Mosaic/Bolton Wanderers deal is probably the most classic example of a football club using a 'clean' shell company to reverse into. Mosaic was identified as a shell company in the *Shell Company Research* newsletter (now part of the *Small Company Selector* newsletter) in December 1995 at 31p. The company was principally a holding company with £9m in cash and operated just one small business making spirit measures and other bar products. Rumours began to surround the company in March 1997 and the company requested its shares be suspended at 51.5p on 6 March in anticipation of an acquisition. The target turned out to be Bolton Wanderers Football & Athletic Company in an offer valuing the club at £22m – payable in new shares. The enlargement of Mosaic's share capital gave Bolton's owners a 67% stake in the new company, providing them with overall control, plus the use of Mosaic's cash pile to help fund the club's impending move to a new stadium and its promotion to the Premier League for the 1997/98 season. The shares were relisted on 1 May 1997 and finished the day at 59p.

The wave of interest in reverse takeovers of soccer clubs is now beginning to be exploited. Soccer Investments plc is a shell company which has been created simply as a vehicle for a football club with stockmarket aspirations to reverse into. The company is advised by Apax Partners, which was instrumental in the reversal of Sheffield United into Conrad. If, within two years, the company has been unsuccessful in finding a suitable team, the shareholders have the option of a cash exit. If the company is successful, it would not be surprising to see clones of Soccer Investments arrive on the market.

CHARTS

Some investors swear by the efficacy of chartist techniques, whilst others swear at them. The use of graphs and complicated pattern analysis to learn about investors' behaviour and likely behaviour has long been a matter of debate, one still unresolved. Charts, like statistics, can be used as a drunkard uses a lampost – for support rather than illumination – but a reasonable compromise is to use them as part of a balanced analytical armoury. Charts are a methodical tool in the same way as a set of accounts, and how much weight you choose to give their findings is a matter of personal choice.

There are a number of charts scattered throughout this book, lending credence to the old adage that a picture is worth a thousand words. Charts are useful to gain a quick overview of a share's history, its trading range, its volatility, its support levels, its resistance levels, and perhaps some idea of how far it might go. Chartism is a subject which has been covered in great detail in a number of specialist books, including *Charters on Charting* (0 948035 21 8 Batsford Business Books), which is packed full of valuable guidance.

Beyond the use of the actual plotted share price as a tool to provide information, chartists have developed numerous complex mathematical charts to help provide information on the timing of buying and selling. Again, many analysts disregard these tools, but others argue that they become self fulfilling if enough chartists follow the same discipline. Among these more esoteric tools are charts such as moving averages which plot the average of a company's share price over a specific period. This has the effect of smoothing out the underlying graph. Chartists often use two moving averages with different periods plotted on the same axis. Apparently, if the longer dated moving average graph has turned upwards and the shorter dated graph turns upwards through the longer dated line, this is known as a 'golden cross'. This is regarded as a strong buying signal. If the lines are heading downwards this is regarded as a sell signal.

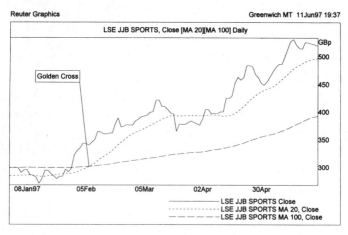

Figure 5.4: Example of Golden Cross (source: Reuters)

Many other tools exist, including (i) relative strength lines which show whether the underlying shares are overbought or oversold (expensive or cheap); (ii) stochastics offer another form of moving average to select buying and selling points; (iii) momentum shows whether the current trend in the chart has enough momentum to carry on its current path, or whether it is likely to peter out; (iv) the moving average convergence/divergence (MACD) uses exponential moving averages to provide overbought/oversold signals above and below a zero line. Again, an upward crossing of the two lines is seen as positive for the share price and a downward one is negative. Crossing of the zero line is confirmation of the change in trend; and (v) candlesticks are a Japanese designed charting tool which uses the opening, closing and intra-day price ranges to determine a trend in the share price.

PERKS

A small additional reason for selecting one share over another may be the existence of some modest shareholder 'perks'. These are rarely of great significance, but they might just tip the balance of the argument in favour of one investment in preference to others on your shortlist. Unfortunately, few sports companies offer perks to shareholders, and buying Manchester United shares will not help you to get match tickets, but there are a couple of companies which extend a hand of welcome – check the company's annual report for details.

PGA European Tour Courses, for example, has introduced special membership terms for shareholders. They can gain playing rights at seven top PGA European Tour courses and a range of other benefits for £130, with the membership extended from a year to eighteen months. This perk may appeal to keen golfers who find themselves in the Algarve, Northampton, London, Stuttgart, Stockholm, or Dublin.

DEALING SPREADS

One common bone of contention amongst many investors is the dealing spread, or the difference between the buying and selling prices. This is often perceived to be so wide as to discourage dealing, although in most cases it is quite fair. The dealing spread is covered in more detail in Chapter 6, but certain factors can contribute to the selection process and even the timing of an investment. For example, a share consolidation which may reduce the dealing spread can provide a signal for investors to buy where previously they may have steered clear.

FUTURE INDUSTRY DEVELOPMENTS

One of the single largest factors driving sports shares higher is the prospect of future industry developments. The major event is the introduction of Pay-Per-View television and this will not only affect the sports clubs. Sportswear retailers may be expected to do more business, as will the manufacturers. But investors must be aware that negative factors can also affect the performance of individual companies and entire sectors. Zetters Group, for example, which principally operates in the football pools industry, has been badly hit by the introduction of the National Lottery. From a high of 147p in September 1994 the shares dropped 38% to 90.5p within three years following an alteration in people's betting habits. Those casual gamblers who belonged to pools syndicates, or simply used the same numbers each week, have switched to the lottery, slashing sales of pools coupons. This is a classic example of political intervention in the markets and this is just one of many factors which can affect the sports industry.

CONCLUSION

Investment in sports companies is, in many ways, much like any other form of investment and must be researched thoroughly. However, as the above sections show, certain specific tools can be used to help choose the correct company. Whether it is a complex mathematical calculation of a football club's potential revenue from PPV, or an educated decision on the future of a new 'xtreme' sport, it is important to analyse all the available information on a company and its market to help make the correct choice for your portfolio.

6

CHAPTER SIX – DEALING IN SPORTS SHARES

Thousands of sports fans who faithfully watch their clubs every week already have an emotional stake in their teams. Fans often feel a considerable sense of loyalty, belonging and ownership, and many would probably like to take a modest financial stake in their club to cement their association. This makes a great deal of sense when, as a supporter, you can have an intimate knowledge of how the business is run and how successful it is. But how can you invest? This is the point at which many potential investors are deterred. If you are not schooled in the art of stockmarket dealing and do not have a stockbroker, the 'system' can seem daunting. How do you buy and sell shares? How do you find a stockbroker? How do you follow the price? What happens if the club is not fully listed on the Stock Exchange? The answer to each of these questions is quite simple, and we explain the procedures in this chapter. In the beginning your best approach will be to keep matters simple: to find a stockbroker and begin trading in Stock Exchange-listed shares. Soon you will find that as you become more absorbed in the subject, so other avenues to profit will present themselves.

For more experienced investors, much of this information will already be familiar and may be too introductory in tone. There are still questions to be answered though. Which stockbrokers have particular knowledge of sports shares? Can unlisted sports companies be bought through the 'over-the-counter' system? Can I buy warrants or other geared instruments on the sector? What about spread betting?

FINDING A STOCKBROKER

Your first step is to find a stockbroker through whom you can buy and sell. There are basically two distinct types: execution only, and advisory. Which you choose depends on what you are seeking, and there is no rule about which is better. On the one hand, first-time investors may have a greater need for the advice and assistance an advisory broker can give; on the other hand, novice investors' dealings are likely to be simpler and of a relatively modest value, making the cheaper execution-only services attractive. For experienced investors who know what they are doing, advice from a stockbroker may be considered superfluous, but when trading in more esoteric instruments their dealing skills can add value.

Low-cost dealing services start from around £7.50 per trade, and are offered by a wide range of firms. These include Sharelink, NatWest's Brokerline, Midland's Teletrade, Investorlink, CaterDeal, and others which you will see advertising regularly in the financial press. There can be important differences in the speed of dealing they offer, and you should insist on instant dealing, but otherwise they are fairly similar in their services. Their low charges mean that you can invest as little as £250 without seeing a large proportion of your money swallowed up by fees.

Of course what all investors really want is lots of help and advice for a minimal charge, but you get what you pay for. Advisory stockbrokers have higher rates of commission, and justify these with services which they will claim are superior. To be fair, they often are. There is a lot of skill involved in being a good stockbroker, both in terms of achieving better prices when you are trading, and in terms of access to placings, new issues, and other offerings.

SPECIALIST STOCKBROKERS

There is no such thing as a dedicated sports stockbroker, but some firms do have far greater expertise than others. One way of measuring this is from their research output. Greig Middleton has, as a firm, devoted some resources specifically to the football sector, and publishes an annual *Football Industry Review* which contains excellent detailed analysis. The firm also acts as stockbroker to some of the clubs listed, notably Celtic and Preston North End. Analyst Nick Batram is considered an authority on the sector and is often quoted in press articles. He writes regular research notes which will be available for clients. The firm has a number of regional offices, and the main London address is given in the Appendix.

One problem with 'star' analysts, beyond their propensity to play the transfer market and move around frequently, is that they can be somewhat aloof from private investors. In many ways it is better to establish a personal relationship with a dealer-stockbroker who may well have access to industry research reports in any case. It is possible to find talented individuals within stockbroking firms with an enthusiasm for the sector, but investors tend to come across these brokers by chance. Mr Colin Smart of Walker, Crips, Weddle, Beck has recently devoted part of his regular news sheet to the sports sector and has developed an interest in these companies. Similarly, Mr Harold Nass of Keith Bayley Rogers has a long-held interest in sports companies which stems partly from his own leisure interests and connections.

Recognising the difficulty which many private investors have in finding a stockbroker, The McHattie Group runs a free *Which Stockbroker* service for its clients which tries to match their requirements to a suitable stockbroker. Many private investors may find this service of use.

BUYING AND SELLING

Once you have a stockbroker, how does the process of buying and selling actually work? You may be surprised by how simple it all is. Once you have set up an account, just telephone your broker and give him your instructions. Detail which shares you wish to buy, and how many, and he or she will transact the business for you. A contract note will be sent within 24 hours confirming the transaction, and you will be required to pay ('settle') within a week. When you are ready to sell, the process works in reverse, and there is little more to it than that. If in doubt, your stockbroker will usually be happy to explain the procedure. There is also an introductory guide called *Share Ownership for All* available from the London Stock Exchange, or summarised on the internet at http://www.londonstockex.co.uk.

TYPES OF LISTING

Most shares have what is termed a 'full' listing on the London Stock Exchange, which means that they have satisfied all of the Exchange's requirements. Many new issues now coming to the market start with the AIM, however, where the costs are much lower. The Alternative Investment Market (AIM) was established in 1995 by the London Stock Exchange for use by smaller companies which may not fulfil the more rigorous demands of the main market. The listing requirements are less onerous, and for this reason the risk is higher. Readers wishing to know more should take a look at Michael Walters' book, *How to Make a Killing in the AIM* (Rushmere Wynne), which carries plenty of detail and examples.

THE OVER-THE-COUNTER MARKET

You can even buy shares in clubs which do not yet have a Stock Exchange quotation. Stockbrokers Brewin Dolphin make prices in several football clubs which are not listed companies but where the shares can still be traded. Arsenal, Everton, Liverpool, and West Ham United are traded in this way, but there are plenty of extra risks you should be aware of before dealing. The key one is that dealing can be far more difficult outside the structure of the Stock Exchange, and that you may not be able to sell when you want to. Some execution-only stockbrokers will not deal on what is termed the 'over-the-counter' market, but a full service broker should be able to do so without any difficulty. If you do consider dealing in these clubs, it is sensible to discuss it first with your stockbroker.

DEALING SPREADS

When you trade in shares you will find that there is a selling price (the bid price) and a buying price (the offer price). The difference between the two is known as the 'spread', and is an important component of the costs involved in trading. Normally, the spread will vary between about 2% and 10% of the share price, but it depends upon the size of the company and the frequency of trading. Some examples are given below:

Table 6.1: Typical dealing spreads, London Stock Exchange, June 1997	
	Bid-Offer
Blacks Leisure	488p-490p
British Bloodstock	85p-92p
Chelsea Village	108p-112p
PGA European	6.5p-7p
Sunderland	385p-395p
Tottenham Hotspur	100p-103p
Windsor	11p-13p

Watch out for the dealing spread on low-priced 'penny' shares. It can be wide. Most of the time you will not find the dealing spread an issue, but on occasions it can prove an intractable problem, although this occurs only in exceptional cases. West Bromwich Albion football club is a rare example of a wide dealing spread which renders trading impracticable:

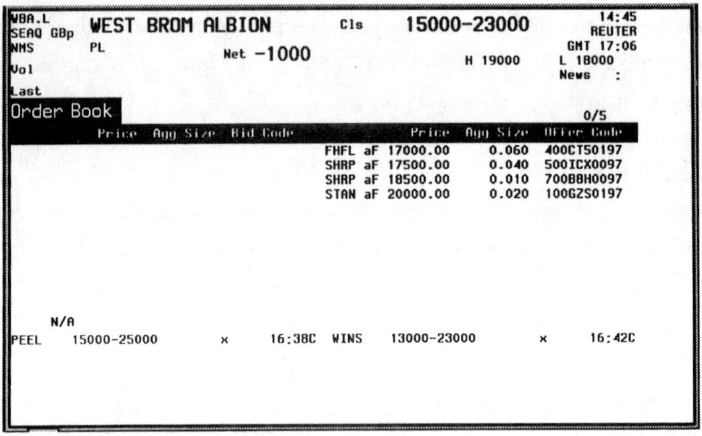

```
WBA.L                                          14:45
SEAQ GBp   WEST BROM ALBION      Cls  15000-23000    REUTER
NMS        PL                                  GMT 17:06
Vol                  Net -1000         H 19000  L 18000
Last                                           News  :
Order Book                                     0/5
         Price  Agg Size  Bid Code       Price  Agg Size  Offer Code
                                FHFL aF 17000.00  0.060  400CT50197
                                SHRP aF 17500.00  0.040  500ICX0097
                                SHRP aF 18500.00  0.010  700B8H0097
                                STAN aF 20000.00  0.020  100GZS0197




      N/A
PEEL    15000-25000      x    16:38C  WINS  13000-23000     x    16:42C

```

Figure 6.1: West Bromwich Albion SEAQ screen quote
(source: Reuters)

Here, the £80 dealing spread (£150-£230) means that the share must rise by this amount – equivalent to 35% of the share price – before holders can break even, not to mention make any profit. This is clearly not acceptable, and is a great big pitfall you will wish to avoid.

TRADING DIFFICULTIES

Larger investors may occasionally encounter problems when wishing to invest large sums of money in small companies. This should not really come as a surprise, but brokers often find their clients expressing anger and bewilderment at finding their money is seemingly not welcome. Of course it is a purely practical matter. The market-makers who set prices and conclude the deals which stockbrokers propose are charged with the task of balancing supply and demand, and to do this they must have what they call a 'normal market size'. This is not usually too small, but it is a factor to be aware of on some occasions. The figures given in the list below are the amounts in which the market-maker is actually obliged to deal, and in many cases you will be able to deal in larger size.

Table 6.2: samples of dealing sizes on the London Stock Exchange, June 1997				
Company	Market Capitalisation	Price	Market Size	Amount
CCI Holdings	£1.42m	177.5p	1,000	£1,775
Hay & Robertson	£31.3m	152.5p	2,500	£3,812
JJB Sport	£379.4m	421.5p	3,000	£12,645
Loftus Road	£24.1m	65p	5,000	£3,250
Newcastle United	£181.6m	127p	25,000	£31,750

You will see that it is easier to invest larger sums in larger companies, particularly when these are actively traded, such as Newcastle United.

FOLLOWING THE PRICE

Unlike engineering firms, retailers, investment trusts, and many other sectors, sports shares do not have a separate prices section in newspapers at present. This may change, but for the moment, investors must embark on a foray through the sections devoted to leisure and hotels, media, AIM, and sometimes others to find the latest prices. This is not too arduous a task once you know where to look, and many investors find it a great pleasure every morning to scour the price pages of their newspaper to check on their favourites. Many prices may also be found on teletext, on the internet, or from a wide range of other sources now available.

ADJUSTMENTS

In February 1997 Tottenham Hotspur's share price went from 600p to 120p overnight. Was there a disaster? No. The explanation was simply that the shares were sub-divided into five to make the price seem less daunting, and shareholders were given five times the number of shares. Of course in reality it makes no difference whether a share happens to be priced at 600p or 6p, but there is a common belief that shares over 500p or so are less marketable. There is no need to worry if a company in which you hold shares proposes a sub-division or some other change along similar lines: they are obliged to treat you fairly and to make sure you do not lose out. Moreover, there is usually a good reason for the change which may enhance the value of your holding.

Another share adjustment you are likely to encounter as a shareholder in fast-growing sports companies is a rights issue. Firms make rights issues when they wish to raise fresh capital, and they will offer shareholders new shares, usually at a price less than the market price. Whether or not you take up the offer depends upon the individual circumstances, and you will receive weighty documents explaining the reasons to help you make up your mind. If you are not sure, and you have an advisory stockbroker, he or she should be able to help.

COLLECTIVE INVESTMENT SCHEMES

For investors who are not confident of their ability to pick winners from the scores of sports shares available, there are collective funds around to spread your risk. Probably the best known is Momentum Premier Sports Partners, which was launched in May 1996. Investing globally, this fund managed 48% growth in its assets in its first 12 months. There are, however, drawbacks for UK investors. The fund is dollar-denominated, based in Bermuda, listed on the Irish Stock Exchange, and has a large minimum investment of US$25,000.

February 1997 saw the launch of the Singer & Friedlander Football Fund to great media interest. Singer & Friedlander is a merchant bank which has been operating since 1907. It is listed on the London Stock Exchange and has around £4bn of funds under management. The bank has acted as an adviser or broker to Southampton, Sheffield United, Tottenham Hotspur, and five other clubs, so it has some pedigree in the field. The group also developed 'Transflo' to assist clubs in dealing with the increasing cost of player transfers, and in 1996 concluded deals for 45% of Premier League clubs and 25% of all 92 football league clubs.

As the name suggests, the fund invests in UK and European football clubs, plus football-related businesses such as stadia, clothing, equipment and media. The fund also invests in potential new issues.

The Football Fund attracted over £30m initially, mainly from around 20,000 private investors. Listed daily in the *Financial Times* 'Managed Fund Service' under 'Offshore and Overseas, Ireland (SIB recognised)', the fund is an open ended collective investment scheme incorporated in Ireland. If the offshore structure worries some investors, the fund has been recognised by the Securities and Investments Board under section 86(2) of the Financial Services Act, and the Investors Compensation Scheme applies for investors buying through Singer & Friedlander Investment Funds Ltd. Cancellation rights do not apply.

The minimum initial investment in the fund is £1,000, or monthly savings start at £50 per month, and investors buying for the first time need to complete an application form. After that, you can deal by telephone or by fax if you wish, confirming it in writing with a cheque within seven days. You will then receive a contract note within a couple of days, and an ownership confirmation within 21 days of payment. When selling you should receive payment about seven working days after your sale. The fund has a single price based on the net asset value rather than a bid-offer spread, but for purchases a charge of 4.5% is added to the price. There is also an annual management fee of 1.5%. Holders receive an annual and half-yearly report.

More funds are likely to emerge as the sector grows in popularity, and it can make good sense for investors to have at least a portion of their money professionally managed. It is less fun than picking your own shares, but it is safer and removes the need for you to keep an eye on your investments all the time.

COVERED WARRANTS

For investors seeking high-risk exposure, Nomura International has been active in the 'covered' warrants market, introducing two series of warrants on the football sector and two on individual clubs. Covered warrants are securities issued by a third party, in this case Nomura, which confer the right to buy a share or other instrument at a fixed price at a specific time in the future.

Nomura has issued warrants on Tottenham Hotspur, Manchester United, and on two football indices. There are also warrants on BSkyB, and as the UK covered warrants market is being lent considerable legitimacy by the London Stock Exchange in 1997, it is possible it may gain a wider popularity. A new screen-based trading system is being established which should make dealing much easier and much more visible.

Investors need to be aware that warrants are high risk instruments where prices can move rapidly and valuations can change dramatically. This can be both rewarding and exciting, but unless you are an expert you should certainly seek advice before taking the plunge. The monthly newsletter *Covered Warrants Alert* provides regular advice and guidance on covered warrants, together with factual information on warrants and their terms.

UNQUOTED COMPANIES

Some sports organisations, run as private companies, can offer shares to members even though the shares may not be tradeable or listed on any exchange. As long as the club is a public limited company (plc), it can make such share offers. Cardiff Rugby Football Club was the first Welsh rugby club to incorporate at the start of 1997, and sought to raise funds to ensure it remained among the elite of European club rugby. A prospectus was issued offering 4m ordinary shares at £1 each, but the offer was only open to members of the holding company, Cardiff Athletic Club.

SPREAD BETTING

An alternative to what are broadly termed 'securities' – shares, trusts, options and warrants – is spread betting, which is becoming increasingly popular. Ladbrokes, William Hill, Sporting Index, City Index and IG Index all offer account facilities to punters keen to back their judgements. Spread betting is what Ladbrokes call "the most exciting, new challenge in betting", and "the betting phenomenon of the nineties". Marketing hyperbole aside, they have a point.

When operating a spread bet you bet higher (buy) or lower (sell) than the bookmakers' spread, which is the range within which they believe the result will fall. An example should make this clearer:

It is the first day of a Test Match between England and Australia. England have won the toss and are to bat first. A spread is offered on England's first innings total. The bookmakers predict England will score between 300 and 320 runs. They quote their spread at 300-320. If you believe they will score more than 320 runs, you bet higher and decide how much to stake per run. If you bet £1 per run, then for every run England score over 320 you win £1. For every run England score below 320, you lose £1. You could sell if you were pessimistic, but on the assumption that you bought and that England scored 370 runs, you would win £50 (370 – 320) x your stake (£1).

Source: *Ladbroke Sporting Spreads*

One key point to be aware of is that, unlike standard fixed-odds betting, you can lose more – much more – than your stake. Had England scored only 250 runs in the example above, you would have lost £70 compared with your stake of £1 per run, so be careful.

Bookmakers offer a very wide range of spread bets on sporting events, and the range is constantly changing. Over one weekend in 1997, for example, the following fascinating array of bets were among those offered by IG Index:

Courage League (Rugby Union) final positions

Weekend rugby match results with time of first try etc

Pilkington Cup Final (Rugby Union) result, and Silk Cut Challenge Cup (rugby league) result

Biggest winning margin in the day's Ascot races

Argentine Grand Prix positions

Formula One Constructors' championship index

Horse racing at Musselburgh and Southwell

US Masters (golf) positions

Premier League (soccer) points total, top London club, top Northern club

Premier League (soccer) top scoring striking partnership

FA Cup and Coca-Cola Cup (soccer) results

European Cup, Cup Winners Cup and UEFA Cup (soccer) results

Tennents Scottish Cup (soccer) results

FA Cup semi-finals, time of first goal, total goals, total bookings, time of first throw-in, total corners etc

Not all of these bets are simple spreads. There are supremacy bets which consider the difference between two teams, performance spreads which are based on compound performance indicators, and some which are more esoteric, such as the "Stop at a Winner" horse racing bet, which is based on a points system. Essentially, you have to decide which will be the first race on the card to be won by the favourite, and the number of points increases by ten each time a race is run, until the favourite wins. For example, if the first two favourites lose but the favourite in the third race wins, then the points total is 30. You may gather from this that sports spread betting is intended to be fun, and that is probably its principal purpose, but it can on occasions fit within a stretched definition of 'investment'.

As an investment area, spread betting is regulated by the Securities and Futures Authority, and you will need to open an account with the bookmaker much as you do with a stockbroker. Once your account is established you can check the 'prices' on teletext or another source, or telephone for quotes, and then place your bets by telephone. Once a bet is open, you do not have to wait for the final conclusion of the sporting event for the outcome. One benefit of spread betting against fixed odds betting is that you can close your position as events develop. Returning to the cricketing example, if England get off to a good start and confidently score 50 runs without losing a wicket, the bookmaker may revise his price to, say, 390-410, and you could choose to close your position bought at 320, pocketing your £70 profit (390 − 320).

This flexibility is a key attraction of spread betting, which allows you to take positions on a broad array of sports and opportunities. It is also effectively tax free, since capital gains tax does not apply to bets, and the betting tax is taken care of in the bookmaker's spread.

WHEN TO BUY AND SELL

There is no simple rule to apply to your investments when deciding when to buy and when to sell. You have to gauge the circumstances of each situation and act accordingly. Some commentators will swear by moving averages, stop-loss systems, or other filters which seek to lend an air of objectivity, but investing is an art, not a science, and decisions are subjective.

For novices in particular, one of the obvious buying opportunities occurs when a company is first 'floated' on the stock market. Completing an application form in the prospectus and sending it off with your cheque is an appealingly simple way of buying shares. No stockbrokers are involved, no commissions are payable, there is no dealing spread, and no fuss. There are, however, complications. First, you will not necessarily be able to gain access to the better quality offerings. Companies are no longer obliged to offer their shares to the public through an 'offer for subscription', and they can instead opt for a 'placing' where the shares are placed privately. It is not usually possible to gain access to placings as a private individual, although preferential treatment is often given to season ticket holders or club members. The flotation of Newcastle United in early 1997 was fairly typical. In this case the company was valued at £193m through its flotation at 135p, but only 40m shares were issued, the remainder being held by existing shareholders. Of those 40m shares, some 85% were then allocated to institutional investors, whose deep pockets ensure they are always at the head of the queue. The remainder was oversubscribed by five times. Preferential applications were met up to £20,000, season ticket holders who applied for shares were allocated around £500 each, and 14,000 members of the public who were not season ticket holders received no shares at all. This last category included television pundit Alan Hansen, whose application for 25,000 shares was booted straight back.

Another problem with new issues is that they are sometimes overpriced. In essence what the company is doing is selling a part of its business, and of course it will wish to do this when its value is high. Unfortunately, the best time for a company to float on the stockmarket will not necessarily be the best time to buy, and history is littered with examples. To take just one, Aston Villa football club was floated at 1100p at the start of May 1997 and ended the month at 830p. Again, there is no general rule here, and each flotation should be judged individually. At least the prospectus will give you plenty of information on which to form an opinion, and as you read more of these documents you will gain some impression of what to look for.

Newspaper and newsletter tips can provide guidance on what to buy, and when, but it is still wise to take some care. One problem which can arise when widely-read publications recommend shares is that the price will rise before you have a chance to deal. For this reason, if following a 'tip' you should always check the price before dealing, and reconsider your purchase if the price has already moved up substantially. If leaving an order with your stockbroker it can be prudent to set a 'limit' price, which is the maximum price at which you are prepared to buy.

When selling, many investors find it extremely hard to accept a loss, but it can be much better to sell at a small loss than to wait and watch it grow into a large loss. This does not necessarily mean that you were wrong to buy, just that new circumstances have arisen which have changed the outlook for the worse. You can only form decisions based on the information you have at a given moment, and sometimes new factors will arise which change your mind. A good example is provided by the *Sports Shares* newsletter, which recommended the shares of sports insurance broker Windsor at 20p in December 1996. The shares rose initially, but when chief executive Michael Eagles resigned in January it became clear that all was not well. In May the newsletter recommended holders sell at 15p and accept a 25% loss, which on the face of it was not a good outcome. When the shares fell to 12p a month later the advice looked a little better.

One method for ensuring losses are kept small is to run what is called a 'stop-loss' system, where you will automatically sell if the price falls by a certain amount, typically 15%-20%. The idea is to nip losses in the bud before they become too large, but to let your profits run and build up. This is a sensible approach, and appealing in its simplicity, but it can be awkward to administer. You will not generally be able to persuade your stockbroker to run a stop-loss on your behalf, so you will have to monitor prices yourself. In volatile markets it can be difficult to operate the system efficiently, and if prices are prone to swing in a wide range, such that a drop of 15% is not necessarily indicative of a downtrend, then the whole system may become error-prone. Again, there is no easy answer.

Finally, when should you take profits when your holdings have soared in value? If you are lucky enough to hold shares which have doubled in value, then it can be sensible to sell half at this time, pocket your original investment, and effectively run the other half for 'free'. Generally, however, it is best to monitor your holdings regularly and to keep up some form of regular analysis (or regular advice) to gauge when to buy or sell. There is no 'quick fix' and no substitute for the detailed forms of analysis covered in Chapter 5.

CONCLUSION

There are numerous ways to deal in sports shares or other instruments, and to back your knowledge and judgement, or merely your prejudices. The popularity of sports shares is well known, but as an example it is worth taking a look at stockbrokers' documented experiences. In the last quarter of 1996 the large execution-only stockbroker Sharelink detailed the top 20 purchases by clients. Big names such as British Telecom, Eurotunnel and Marks and Spencer dominated the list, of course, but there were also four sports shares in the top 20. Blacks Leisure was 12th, followed by Caspian Group, Chelsea Village and Manchester United. Lots of private investors deal in sports shares regularly, and it is not difficult once you know what you are doing. Do not be deterred by apparent complications, or worry about sounding ignorant if you are unsure. Ask people who know, and they will generally be glad to explain queries.

7

CHAPTER SEVEN – OVERSEAS OPPORTUNITIES

Sport is of course a worldwide phenomenon, and so is investment in sport. And just as British football clubs have often found overseas players to be better buys, so may British investors find overseas companies more attractive. Dealing in overseas shares can be more expensive, but it is possible, and through business or family connections you may acquire some special knowledge of an overseas sport which you wish to exploit. This chapter mentions a few specific investments, but there are thousands more which receive little attention and which may hide untapped value.

Even if you have no intention whatsoever of buying any overseas shares, it can be useful to study the companies. There are lessons to be learned from trends in other countries. Take, for example, the case of Stockholm ice hockey team Djurgarden, which hopes to become the first sports club to list in Sweden late in 1997. This serves as a useful reminder that ice hockey can be a leading, popular sport, and that we could see similar listings in the UK in due course. Investors with access to the internet can follow the progress of teams such as the Sheffield Steelers (http://www.steelers.co.uk), and may be surprised by the crowd sizes. Overseas travel is said to broaden the mind: so does consideration of overseas investments.

The other point of relevance when considering overseas companies relates to international competition. Multi-national companies can decide to come and compete for market share in a local economy where one firm may previously have been dominant. An example is Sports Authority, one of the world's leading sporting goods retailers which operates in the US, Canada and Japan. Capitalised at US$580m, Sports Authority has the muscle to move into Europe and is already considering moves into Germany. If and when the company shifts its attention to the UK, shareholders in retailers Blacks Leisure, JJB Sports and John David Sports may wish they knew more about the newcomer.

AMERICAN SPORTS

Outside the UK, there is only one country which has a large number of listed sports companies. It is the United States, where sport is virtually a national religion. It is also of course a realm peculiar to the US: for all the pretence of the 'World Series', baseball, basketball and American football are not played extensively elsewhere, and there is no sense in which any of these sports can be regarded as world games as soccer may. This insularity can mean that overseas investors never consider the US sports teams which have quotations, or the companies which make sporting goods specifically for the domestic market. Yet they are interesting.

Boston Celtics is a professional basketball team which plays in the National Basketball Association (NBA). The Celtics' business is analogous in many ways to soccer teams in the UK, with the majority of revenue coming from ticket sales (54%), television rights (34%) and merchandising and advertising (12%). And its performance on the market has a strong link to its performance on the court. Formed in 1946 and taken public 40 years later, Boston Celtics is probably the most successful NBA team in history, with 16 titles and 17 players in the hall of fame, but the lustre has faded and the team has not won the title for a decade. The 90,000 or so investors in the company have not seen a return to make them jump. The shares reached US$18.38 as long ago as 1987, and ended 1996 at US$22.25, so this could prove a salutary tale for investors considering football clubs. Success today need not mean success tomorrow.

Ackerley Group Inc owns the Seattle Supersonics NBA team, amongst other things. The links are interesting, because the company is also involved with billboard advertising and media (television and radio stations), both allied businesses to some degree. The company is certainly well aware of spin-offs and secondary marketing, and has expanded its interests in such periphery as food concessions and retail sales of sporting goods since it acquired the Supersonics in 1983.

Another diversified sporting club listed is the Florida Panthers. The Panthers are a professional ice hockey team playing in the National Hockey League (NHL). Far from being a pure team play, however, the company also has a majority stake in the Miami Arena stadium where the Panthers play, and has diversified into the hotel and resort industry. The billionaire H Wayne Huizenga has said that "we plan to build it into a very aggressive company", which somehow seems appropriate for an ice hockey franchise.

Of course American football is the greatest spectator sport in the US, and the January 1997 Super Bowl set a new record for the sales of merchandise. The Green Bay Packers 35-21 win over the New England Patriots generated US$130m in Super Bowl merchandise sales, comfortably beating the 1996 record of US$100m. According to figures from the National Football League (NFL) it is the Dallas Cowboys who lead the league in merchandise sales.

The same team leads the table of US sports franchise values compiled by *Financial World* magazine in 1997. The Cowboys are estimated to be worth US$320m, well above the average franchise value for American football of US$205m. Basketball franchises work out at an average value of US$148m, baseball at US$134m, and ice hockey at US$90m. What is perhaps most interesting is that no US sports franchise approaches the value of Manchester United, which may say something about the latter's international appeal.

In time, it may be Major Soccer League teams who head the tables for world sales of soccer goods, as the ambitious US administrators of the sport have great hopes. "Our goal is to win the World Cup by

2010," deputy commissioner Sunil Gulati told the SoccerEx 97 conference, conceding that work was still to be done. "The goal is to be one of the five major US sports," he added. For the moment, American football, ice hockey, baseball and basketball are well ahead, and manufacturers of specialist equipment for these American sports have their own niche. To name just two, Riddell Sports makes football helmets and protective athletic equipment; and Rawlings Sporting Goods makes baseball equipment and uniforms. Rawlings was hit of course in 1994-95 when US baseball players went on strike for an entire season, which is a reminder that even the most well-established of sports can suddenly run into trouble.

GOLF

Golf is a heavily brand-sensitive game, perhaps more than many investors realise. Leading player Tiger Woods is sponsored by Nike, which does not even make golf products, to the tune of US$40m, now considered a bargain in light of his growing status. The perception of the game as a technical challenge where players can be aided by special, hi-tech, up-to-date equipment also helps manufacturers to sell large numbers of clubs, balls, and gadgets. Annual golf club sales in the US alone are steady at around US$23.3m per year, and other markets such as Japan are also important. Mizuno Corporation is the largest comprehensive manufacturer of sporting goods in Japan, and is best known for its golfing goods. Capitalised at ¥88,421m (£430m), it has overseas subsidiaries in Taiwan, France, UK, US, and Mexico.

Callaway Golf Company, which is based in California, makes one of the most well-known clubs with the pithy name 'Big Bertha'. Big Bertha is named after the German World War I howitzers which could hit enemy targets at a range of 76 miles. Launched in 1991, the Big Bertha driver is ranked number one by usage on the five major golf tours and has elevated Callaway to the top spot in golf club manufacture in the US. Its growth has certainly been impressive: net sales have leapt from US$21.5m in 1990 to US$553m in 1996, and earnings per share have risen from US$0.04 to US$1.73 over the same period. The company is now capitalised at US$2.4bn (£1.5bn), and is considered the leader in its sector. Founder Ely Callaway has rightly been credited with an innovative mind coupled with great marketing sense

Figure 7.1: Callaway Golf Company share price 1990-97 (source: Bloomberg)

Amongst Callaway's competitors are two companies associated with well-known former champions. Golden Bear Golf Inc, which has the stock exchange ticker symbol 'JACK', is controlled by Jack Nicklaus, and the Arnold Palmer Golf Company should be self-explanatory. There are at least thirty specialist golf companies listed on American stock exchanges, bearing testimony to the popularity of the game and to its commercial success. Some of the stocks are not of the highest quality, however, and Callaway has set a standard which other companies are finding hard to match. Investors have scored a lot of bogies with stocks such as Golden Bear and TearDrop Golf, so watch out for the hazards.

A variation on the golf stocks theme in America is the real estate investment trusts (REITs) which are taking advantage of the growth of around 2,000 'golf communities' which have sprung up over the last fifteen years. These popular schemes feature homes surrounding golf courses and have attracted luminaries such as Tiger Woods and basketball star Shaquille O'Neal. National Golf Properties is the largest golf REIT with 117 courses, recently joined by a smaller competitor, Golf Trust of America.

Finally, and staying with the American market for illustration, there is clothing. You cannot play golf on a decent course in your jeans and trainers. Golf apparel is big business, and is split between specialist companies such as Ashworth (10% owned by golfer Fred Couples), Cutter & Buck and Sport-Haley, and the larger fashion brands which carry a line of golf clothing. Reebok International has a division called the Greg Norman Collection, which markets and distributes men's sportswear and golf apparel.

WINTER SPORTS

French ski manufacturers Groupe Salomon and Ski Rossignol are good examples of how not to pre-judge the relationship between companies and their underlying sports. In some cases it is possible to form a judgement on the growth and popularity of a particular sport and to test your theory by dealing in a company specialising in that sport. In other cases it is not. Industry figures show that worldwide sales of alpine skis fell from 7m pairs in 1991/92 to just 4m pairs in 1996/97, and Ski Industries of America reckons that visits to US ski resorts have not grown in a decade. So do the share price graphs of Salomon and Ski Rossignol look like ski slopes? No.

Figure 7.2: Groupe Salomon share price 1991-97
(source: Bloomberg)

Figure 7.3: Ski Rossignol share price 1991-97
(source: Bloomberg)

The reason is that it is too easy to think of Salomon and Rossignol as pure alpine ski manufacturers. In fact they have both diversified in response to market conditions, and Salomon's winter sports business is expected to drop to below 50% of its turnover in 1997. It is also responding to market demand and changing its product mix to meet customers' requirements. Recognising, for example, that the enthusiasm for traditional skiing is waning in Japan, Salomon has started to ship snowboards. It is planning to deliver 10,000 boards to Japan in 1997 and to double that in 1998. Los Angeles-based K2, another ski manufacturer, has taken this one step, or one run, further, and moved into snowboards, in-line skates, mountain bikes, backpacks, and fishing gear.

Snowboards have, of course, been a great growth niche, but it can prove difficult to translate general trends in sports into stock-specific investment success. It depends upon the individual companies. Morrow Snowboards, for example, which makes 32 models of snowboard plus a range of accessories, has seen its shares slip and slide down from US$16.25 at the end of 1995 to US$5 in early 1997. An even steeper slope was presented to shareholders in Corsaire Snowboards, which was established as a vehicle to acquire snowboard manufacturers. It never did, it ran into a series of legal problems, and the shares slipped right down from US$20 in 1994 to a low of US$1 in early 1995.

In addition to winter sports goods, some skiers can use their knowledge of resorts to make profitable investments. A resort in central western Sweden, Lindvallen I Saelen, made the news in 1997 with an all-stock bid for neighbouring ski resorts Tandaadalen and Hundfjaellet. The largest ski area in the world, the Trois Vallees in France, is partly controlled by the public company Meribel Alpina, which has been listed on the Second Marche in Paris since November 1995 (and on the over-the-counter market for thirty years previously). Lots of British skiers visit the resorts of Meribel, Courchevel, Les Menuires and Val Thorens, and their decisions are based on a range of factors. It is a superb skiing destination, and that is not in doubt, but what about the snowfall? If the snow reports are not good, people will stay away, and in years such as 1989 this has been an intractable problem. Equally, and this has been a relevant factor in recent years, the expense matters, and a key element of this is the exchange rate. The strong French franc has not helped.

In November 1996 the shares of Meribel Alpina dropped 5% when the company revealed a drop in profits of 15% due largely to factors beyond its control. Insufficient snowfall, transport strikes, an economic slowdown, and unfavourable currency movements were blamed, and the real point to note with these is that they are difficult for investors to predict. To some degree you may be able to use your own knowledge of the resort and whether, for example, the operator has been investing in snow-making machinery to lessen its dependence on the weather to a limited extent. Unforeseen factors are always liable to arise, however, making resort operators a relatively high risk investment.

FOOTWEAR: NIKE, REEBOK, ADIDAS

The largest sporting goods manufacturer, with an estimated 43% share of the American sports footwear market, Nike is still exhibiting strong growth on an international basis. In its third quarter 1996/97, revenue leapt by 53% to US$2.4bn, so it is little wonder that analyst Brett Barakett said: "Results like these reinforce that Nike is the dominant player in the industry and reinforces their position as one of the world's great consumer brands." Nike sells its goods in 110 countries around the world, and the company is capitalised at over US$10bn (£6.25bn), making it larger than chemicals giant ICI.

Reebok is paying £2m per year to sponsor Bolton Wanderers' new Burnden Park ground, but is better known as the number two in the US athletic shoe market. Named after a speedy African antelope, the manufacturer of Reebok shoes for adults, and Weebok shoes for kids has been a fabulous success story, though punctuated more recently with disappointments. The company's sales have climbed from US$3.5m in 1982 to US$3,478.6m in 1996, and the shares have jumped from a low of US$4.19 in 1986 to a high of US$52.875 in early 1997. The company has been lagging Nike's recent expansion, and has fallen behind further in market share, but investors do not yet have any burning desire to see chief executive Paul Fireman shot down in flames.

An official sponsor of the 1998 soccer World Cup and generator of no less than DM360m (£129m) of operating profit in 1996, Adidas is also a force to be reckoned with in the world of sports merchandising. Sales in 1996 topped £1.6bn. The shares are listed in Frankfurt, in Deutschemarks, and the company is based in Herzogenaurach in Germany, but it is of course global in its ambitions. The company is currently placed fourth in the lucrative US market, but is seeking to make inroads through new sponsorship. According to the Sporting Goods Manufacturers' Association, sporting goods sales in the US will grow 6.3% to US$44.1bn in 1997, accounting for nearly half of the world market. Adidas sponsors the New York Yankees' baseball team, and shareholders must already feel as though they have hit a home run. Adidas shares have already doubled since their launch at DM68 in November 1995.

ITALIAN FOOTBALL CLUBS

Although this is just hearsay at the time of writing, it does seem that Italian football clubs are likely to seek stockmarket listings in the near future. AC Milan has spoken of a flotation in London or New York, and others such as Bologna, Juventus and Lazio have been mentioned in the same vein. The Milan Stock Exchange, which is perhaps the more obvious starting point, requires companies to have three consecutive years of profits before listing, and sadly the football clubs cannot live up to this requirement. New television rights contracts come into force in 1999 and the clubs are hoping to generate extra revenue from Pay-Per-View thereafter.

Some financial players are already jockeying for position ahead of the flotations. Merrill Lynch (acting for a group of investors) and Bankers Trust each took a 33% stake in second division Torino in March 1997. The catalyst for change came in September 1996, when the government passed new laws to allow teams to make profits and distribute dividends, previously forbidden. As a result the structure of the game is likely to move away from paternalistic owners hoping to bask in the reflected glory of victory. AC Milan, owned by media mogul Silvio Berlusconi, is credited with assisting his campaign to become Prime Minister in 1994. How the success of Juventus may persuade more Italians to buy Fiat motor cars, beyond some huge surge in national pride, is not clear, but corporate ownership is widespread. Parma is owned by dairy company Parmalat, the ERG oil company owns Sampdoria, and the Moratti oil refining family owns Milan's Internazionale. It will be interesting to see whether Italian football clubs follow the lead of British clubs which too were once the domain of wealthy individuals or consortia with a range of non-financial goals.

OTHER OVERSEAS FOOTBALL CLUBS

In Denmark, there is already a listed football sector, although not of a size to rival the UK. Broendby IF, AGF Kontraktfodbold, and SIG Fodbold Support A/S are all listed in Copenhagen, but their combined market capitalisation is relatively modest. Partly because of this, prices can swing wildly on individual results, making them great fun for speculators. When Broendby won the first leg of their UEFA Cup match against Tenerife by 1-0 in March 1997 the shares leapt by 23.7% in one trading session. Then Tenerife won the second leg by 2-0 and Broendby shares fell 15.5% in reaction. Such volatility is not uncommon, and the shares leapt by 45% following the 1996 results which showed a strong rise in profits to Dkr20.9m, a far cry from the dark days of the early 1990s. Broendby suffered from a disastrous foray into banking which should serve as a warning to clubs venturing far from their base business. The story dates back to 1987 when the club's flotation was oversubscribed six times and the club was basking in success both on and off the field. Large transfer fees had swelled the club's finances and within three years the shares had doubled in value. The company then bought Interbank in 1991 and suffered as its shares dipped on bad results, preventing it from raising much-needed cash at a time when it was needed, and this in turn led to a loss of confidence. The shares slumped from Dkr360 to Dkr30, and the club had to be rescued from bankruptcy by a group of finance houses. You have been warned: if Chelsea Village buys the Chelsea Building Society, sell the shares quickly.

French football clubs are pressing for changes in the fiscal rules to allow them to operate more as commercial companies. At present they are not allowed to list on stock exchanges and they cannot pay dividends. As Bernard Brochand, co-chairman of leading club Paris St Germain, has observed: "The French sports structure prevents clubs from being real businesses." The implication of this is that French clubs are finding it more difficult to compete for the best players as European mobility grows. Even after these rules change, as seems likely, the Paris stock market is similar to Milan in requiring three years of profits before companies are eligible.

The Swiss Football Association decided in early 1997 to accept publicly-listed companies in its national league. Zurich Grasshoppers and Geneva's Servette already have a share capital structure, but are not listed. Given that the revenue streams for Swiss clubs are a trickle compared with the open floodgates at big British clubs, investors may prove shy about investing in such clubs as Aarau and Young Boys of Berne, but if Preston North End and West Bromwich Albion can raise finance then it would be unwise to rule it out.

Dutch football clubs seem to be in no rush to flock to the stockmarket. TV rights are not presently negotiated by the clubs, and it could be some time before the revenue flows are high enough to attract investors. Ajax Amsterdam have said that they do not need the capital, but PSV Eindhoven chairman Hans van Raay is aware of the inevitable march of the stockmarket. He says: "Football is becoming increasingly international. You need capital to compete successfully with big clubs elsewhere and the stock market offers the best way to raise it."

Brazilian football clubs are non-profit making organisations at present, but special sports minister and footballing hero Pele is seeking to change their status. He is likely to push through legislation forcing them to restructure as private enterprises and publish their accounts. In due course this could lead to flotations on the burgeoning Brazilian stockmarket, although this may be some way off. The same is true for South African soccer clubs, which are enjoying an influx of cash. In 1996 the country's major cup competition was worth R1.7m, with R200,000 for the winner; in 1997 these figures leapt to R7m and R1.2m respectively. Moreover, oil company Total has signed a R12m (£1.63m) deal with the top club Kaizer Chiefs, so the sport is being propelled into the commercial arena.

US STOCK CAR RACING

Accelerating rapidly into the twenty-first century, stock car racing has been a fast-growing sport in America over recent years. Companies such as International Speedway, Grand Prix of Long Beach, Penske Motorsports, Dover Downs, and Speedway Motorsports trade on high ratings as investors buy in to fast-growing attendances, television receipts, and sponsorship. A report in the American financial weekly Barron's outlined the attractions of the stocks in its March 17th 1997 issue, explaining the history of the sport and how the 30-race Winston Cup circuit pulls great audiences. "Winston Cup ratings are double or triple those of basketball and hockey," the report said, and statistics showed "annual attendance for Winston Cup races growing more than 10% a year for the past few years", with 5.6m paying to see the 1996 races. Fans are wealthy, loyal, receptive to merchandising, and when sponsorship and broadcasting fees are added in the lights have gone green for track companies to make money. Speedway Motorsports was the first to come to the New York Stock Exchange in February 1995 and has more than trebled in value since. The company's president, HA 'Humpy' Wheeler, says: "I don't think there is another sport in the United States that can draw 100,000 fans or more on the kind of consistent basis Nascar can." Other firms have followed, and this is now a sector in its own right which attracts hard-nosed investors as much as race fans.

Figure 7.4: Speedway Motorsports share price 1995-1997 (source: Bloomberg)

A FEW SURPRISING PUBLIC COMPANIES

There is no shortage of 'human interest' material for the sector. Zambian football club Mufulira Wanderers is apparently considering a listing on the Lusaka Stock Exchange, which is perhaps no more strange than West Bromwich Albion being quoted in London, but it can still raise a smile. The Topps Company, which makes 'Bazooka' bubble gum, is on the investment list for one sports fund because it features sports figures on some of its picture cards. Healthsouth Corporation, which runs rehabilitation services for disabled patients and those suffering from stroke, head trauma and other injuries, seems a particularly unlikely candidate for inclusion in the sector. But it has a line in sports medicine and deals with sports-related injuries. In Sweden, a company by the name of Feelgood Svenska came to the stock market in 1997. It provides health, personnel development, rehabilitation and physical therapy services to companies for their staff. Feelgood's sales have grown on average 34% per year for the last ten years, so there is no shortage of feelgood factor about their figures.

There are some pursuits which may almost be labelled 'sports' which are quite country-specific and which may not appear obvious to anyone outside that country. In Japan, for example, Sankyo Company and Heiwa are both makers of pachinko machines. Pachinko is an onomatopoeic word for a noisy variety of pinball, played with ball-bearings which are aimed at certain places, and which when hit will return more balls. This may sound frivolous, but as long ago as 1953 there were 5,000 registered pachinko halls in Tokyo, and probably upwards of 19,000 in Japan now. The industry is estimated to generate billions of pounds in revenue each year, and these two companies are together capitalised at ¥374,719m (£1.8bn). Their combined profits for their latest financial years amount to £296m, which is no mean sum. Pachinko could be the sound of the cash dropping into their coffers.

Names can also be misleading. Sports companies will not necessarily have the word 'sports' or 'club' in their titles. Take, for instance, the People Company Limited, a Japanese public company. An educated guess might place the company as a recruitment consultant, or perhaps some other kind of support service. In fact the People Company operates fitness clubs and swimming, tennis and physical training schools, and was the first company in that sector to go public in Japan.

Even well known brand names can be hidden behind anonymous corporate exteriors. Take the Nordic Track exercise equipment range, for example, manufactured by CML Group Inc. The reason for this is, of course, that the company owns other brands and makes other products besides, including Smith & Hawken stores which sell workwear, gardening tools and plants. One particular conglomerate will raise more eyebrows than any other though. American Brands Inc is a worldwide 'consumer products' company best known for its cigarettes, cigars, smoking tobacco, and distilled spirits – hardly the stuff of healthy living.

Table 7.1: Selected brands of 'sports' company American Brands Inc (source: *Hoover's Handbook*)
Benson & Hedges (cigarettes)
Berkeley (cigarettes)
Silk Cut (cigarettes)
Hamlet (cigars)
Old Holborn (tobacco)
Gilbey's (vodka)
Whyte & Mackay (whiskey)
Cobra (golf clubs)
Foot-Joy (golf shoes)
Titleist (golf equipment)

American Brands is trying to quit smoking and has taken up golf. Starting with the tobacco, the company is spinning off its Gallaher subsidiary which leads UK cigarette sales with a market share of around 40%. This divestment is expected to be completed in 1997. American Brands began to diversify way back in 1966, then waited thirty years before moving into sports. The company bought Cobra Golf for US$700m in 1996, and has found it to be a highly successful brand. Golfing sensation Tiger Woods not only uses Cobra clubs (information on the internet is available on http://www.cobragolf.com), but also uses the company's Titleist balls. The Titleist Professional is apparently of wound, three-piece construction, with a resilient patented Elastomer cover and an aerodynamic design. And it seems to work.

8

CHAPTER EIGHT – THE FUTURE FOR SPORTS SHARES

A Mintel study has shown that in 1995 the private health market generated turnover of around £560m and this is expected to increase by 24% in real terms to the year 2000. Health and fitness clubs are proliferating. Almost all Premiership football clubs are expected to be listed on the London Stock Exchange by the year 2000. Smaller clubs such as Preston North End FC are able to back their ambitions with stockmarket cash. New stadiums are being built by UK soccer clubs unable to accommodate the demand from spectators. Even Wembley stadium is being redeveloped. Pay-Per-View television is coming. Rugby Union has turned professional and the British Lions' side has just agreed to bear shirt sponsorship for the first time. Formula One is on the stockmarket starting grid. Sports retailers are expanding furiously, selling the products of successful merchandising companies. New sports fashions are being generated by huge marketing budgets, and the onslaught of sport in a wide range of different media shows no sign of abating.

The list of reasons for a continuing boom in sport and sports shares is almost endless, and counter-arguments are hard to find. Prince Philip's famous remark in 1981 that . . . "everybody was saying we must have more leisure. Now they are complaining they are unemployed" . . . may have been well wide of the mark, but his first thought was correct. People are making more time for health, fitness, and leisure pursuits, even if this amounts only to spectating. As a result, the companies which provide the products and services for the sector are expanding, making more money, and their shares are performing well. It is no coincidence that the FT Leisure & Hotels Index has outperformed the FT-All Share Index by more than 12% over the last five years, and it can be expected to continue doing so. There is not a dedicated sports index at present to enable a more direct comparison, but this is one development which may well be stimulated by the growth in the sector.

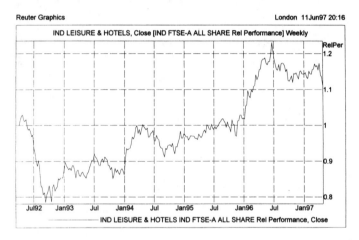

Figure 8.1: Performance of FT Leisure & Hotels Index relative to FT All-Share, 1992-97 (source: Reuters)

CHANGES IN OWNERSHIP

Probably the greatest development which may occur over the next ten years is large corporation ownership of sports clubs. At present, all of the quoted football clubs in the UK are independent companies, mainly of a modest size. What many commentators suggest will happen is that the large leisure groups – Rank Group, Granada Group, Whitbread – or groups from overseas, will seek to buy attractive sporting brands such as Manchester United. Speculation has already arisen, as mentioned in Chapter 5, and it is unlikely to go unfulfilled. There seems much to gain from cross-marketing and cross-selling, and many overseas clubs are already owned by larger companies, including

Italian football club Parma, owned by Parmalat, and the Atlanta Braves baseball team owned by Time Warner Inc. In May 1997, media mogul Rupert Murdoch announced he was negotiating to buy the Los Angeles Dodgers baseball team, noting that "other media companies now in America have great sporting teams". This is not a trend which has hit the UK yet, but is does seem likely that it will, and when it does there could be some considerable profits to be made from the takeover battles.

Another possibility is that cross-border alliances spring up. There has already been talk of a link between Caspian Group, the owners of Leeds United football club, and PSV Eindhoven of the Netherlands. The benefits of sharing players, equity, and business skills are manifest, and there could be plenty of scope for cross-marketing too. The ferocity of supporters allegiances, coupled with the law at present which prevents cross-ownership within the UK, makes it unlikely there will be large sporting conglomerates within this country, but this does not prevent international ties.

POLARISATION

It has already been noted that bidders for sports companies will only fight over the best brands, and one unfortunate consequence of commercialisation generally is that the gap between rich and poor, between winners and losers, will grow. Whereas in the past a team's dominance has usually been the product of some great players or a great manager, transient factors, it is easier now to buy your way to success. Once you have success, it is then easier to maintain it as the virtuous commercial circle of gate money, TV cash and merchandising revenues all flood in. As high-spending Middlesbrough proved in the 1996/97 season, when they were relegated, buying expensive stars does not always work, but most of the time it will. How the smaller clubs grab a slice of the pie is becoming an increasingly vexed question, and the sad fact is that they are likely to find it harder and harder to compete.

Much depends of course on the development of Pay-Per-View television, which is covered in detail in Chapter 3. This is again likely to line the pockets of the large, wealthy clubs at the expense of others, particularly as lack of geographical proximity will no longer be a barrier to watching your favourite team every week. The extension of 'choice' may be welcomed, but the obvious choice for many fans will be to watch Manchester United, Liverpool and Newcastle rather than Swansea, Norwich and Exeter City. Much the same will be true if plans for a European Super-League ever come to fruition. This will provide larger clubs with even more attractive fixtures and even more cash, whilst the minnows will be relegated to the status of 'feeder' clubs, or even disappear altogether. Steps to improve the financial health of the large clubs, and the health of soccer investments, may be quite detrimental to the health of the game overall, and investors will need to guard against short-term gains diminishing the long-term prospects.

LESSONS FROM HISTORY

There are lots of lessons to be learned from what has happened in the past, some positive, some negative. Of course there are long-term trends which mean that some events will never be repeated, but there are also cycles which repeat certain patterns through the generations.

Nowhere is the cyclical pattern more marked than on the catwalk. If you are old enough to remember flared trousers, kipper ties, and wide lapels, then you are old enough and wise enough to know that fashions fade. Yes, Nike trainers and Adidas 'three-stripe' clothing may be in vogue for now, and possibly for some time yet, but not indefinitely. When the change comes, as it surely will, this may hit the market for merchandise sold through specialist retailers, whose heady expansion will run into the wall of full capacity. When it does, you will not want to be holding the shares of sports retailers.

Although supporters may consider this to be football's heyday, a glance at historical records shows it to be otherwise. In terms of crowds at least, even clubs which are successful now have attendance records which dwarf their current capacities. Consider Everton, for example, a moderately successful premiership side with a ground capacity at Goodison Park of 40,200. Their record attendance is 78,229, and a poll of fans at the end of the 1997 season showed that 84% were in favour of a move to a new 60,000-seater stadium away from Liverpool city centre. Coventry City, one of the longest-serving clubs in the top flight, have a current capacity of 23,672 compared with their record of 51,455. What this implies is that crowds could get much larger if grounds were extended (as some such as Old Trafford and Stamford Bridge have been), and that football has not necessarily found its full capacity yet in spite of its seeming popularity.

EMERGING SPORTS

As the years go by, so different sports will wax and wane in their popularity, and some secondary sports will come to the fore, such as ice hockey. Who would have dreamt, in the days of black and white television, that snooker would attract such large audiences and pay out such large sums in prize money to its stars? When Pot Black first came to British television screens in 1969 it would have seemed inconceivable that eighteen years later, a player called Ronnie O'Sullivan could earn £165,000 for just 320 seconds work in compiling a 147 maximum break during the World Championships. Similarly, snowboards are a relatively new phenomenon which have now carved out a prominent position in sales of winter sports equipment, and fitness clubs with user-friendly aerobic equipment are starting to flex their muscles where serious bodybuilders once pumped iron. It is difficult to guess which sports might capture our imagination in the future, but forecasters can find some safer ground amongst established sports which are not yet well represented on the stockmarket. Tennis and fishing are just two popular sports which spring to mind, and which could expand their commercial interests as entrepreneurs look for opportunities outside the fields which have already been well exploited.

More immediately, many observers expect more Rugby Union clubs to come to the stockmarket as professionalism exercises its grip. Anyone who has been to see a club like Bath, one of the leading teams, will know that rugby clubs have a long, long way to travel before they approach the facilities and commercial nous of football clubs. At Bath the small crowd is crammed in, with many standing in rows on a flat surround, peering over the shoulder of the spectators in front. One of the stands looks like a temporary erection. Club colours are scarce among the crowd, who are ironically more able to afford expensive merchandising than most football fans. There is plenty of scope for development, for which funds are of course required. At the present time, Wasps is the only Rugby Union side to be quoted, as part of Loftus Road plc, and it is probably no coincidence that Wasps are the English league champions. Eagles plc, parent company for the Sheffield Eagles Rugby League side, has recently been floated on the AIM, and more rugby clubs can be expected to join the securities scrum over the next few years.

And how about cricket? Surrey county cricket club introduced an innovation at the start of the Sunday league season in 1997 by broadcasting musical accompaniments for incoming batsmen. The new man in can steel his nerves by walking out to the sound of his favourite pop music, which seems an extraordinary contrivance for what is usually a fairly staid sport. The point of mentioning this is that anything is possible, and county cricket clubs could be the commercial stars of tomorrow, even if the odds seem stacked against this possibility now.

POTENTIAL PROBLEMS

On the flip side, and as the US baseball industry has illustrated, all sports can have their problems. As service industries with agent-managed personnel with large pay packets and even larger egos, sports clubs are particularly vulnerable. For a start, their key personnel can misbehave in ways which would seem extremely unlikely (and unbecoming) from the top management, at, say Marks and Spencer. When Manchester United star Eric Cantona launched his now infamous 'kung-fu' kick into the crowd at Crystal Palace on January 25th 1995, the club's shares dropped by 3.8% the following day. When the same player retired unexpectedly in May 1997, £8.7m was wiped off the club's shares. In the same month, newly-floated Heart of Midlothian was forced to sack former French international striker Stephane Paille when he failed a random drugs test, and its shares fell by 2.8%. Nor are these difficulties confined to football, of course. The golfer John Daly lost his lucrative product endorsement contract with Wilson Sporting Goods Co in 1997 after he re-entered alcohol rehabilitation.

If individual petulance and predicaments were not worrying enough, sports players often have a collective voice. Players' unions are widespread, meaning that industries such as football are liable to strikes. If this seems a remote possibility, think again. In the summer of 1996, English soccer players outside of the Premier League were on the verge of a strike over their share of TV revenue. In 1997, Gerardo Movilla, president of the Association of Spanish Footballers, demanded a reduction in the number of foreign players allowed in the Spanish league, and this was after the threat of a stoppage had already been used by the players to create a Christmas break. In October 1996 an Afrikaans newspaper reported claims of an impending player revolt over wages ahead of a rugby tour by the Springboks.

Players' actions can also impinge upon sponsors and merchandising firms. The French Soccer Federation has an exclusive contract until 1998 with Adidas which means that players must wear Adidas boots when playing for their country. Your first thought may well be that this is commercialisation run riot, and that players should wear their normal boots which are comfortable and allow them to perform at their best. Not surprisingly, the same thought has occurred to the players, and captain Didier Deschamps has hinted that players with commitments to rival sports brands may refuse to comply. Player power should not be underestimated.

In case players do not give you enough to worry about, there are team managers too. Their jobs are notoriously lacking in tenure, and the market can take it badly if a manager leaves unexpectedly. A good example is provided by Eagles, the Rugby League side which came to the market in May 1997. The prospectus, published on April 17th, said that: "The directors consider that the new coaching team of Phil Larder and John Kear . . . represent a sound foundation for the future." On 22 May, the day after the club's shares began trading, Phil Larder "agreed to leave the club by mutual consent with immediate effect" and the shares plunged to a 22.5% discount to the 40p offer price. Similarly, when manager Graeme Souness and director of football Lawrie McMenemy resigned from Southampton football club in May 1997 the shares dropped by 10.8% on the following trading day.

Player strikes and manager insecurities aside, consider the following range of problems which could arise. Golf could be hit by one-player dominance lessening interest, by increasing pressures on space restricting the construction of golf courses, or by environmental concerns. Rugby could be destroyed by infighting amongst its administrators as the sport restructures and learns to adapt to professionalism. Horce racing could suffer betting scandals. There have been calls for boxing to be banned following the death of competitors. The same applies to motor racing. Sports retailers are subject to the vagaries of fashion. Betting companies are subject to changes in legislation. The over-riding fact is that no sports company is invulnerable, and that external, uncontrollable factors are always liable to come into play. Take, for example, the election of the new Labour government in the UK in 1997. Within weeks the new administration announced plans to ban all tobacco advertising from sport. Health minister Frank Dobson said "we recognise that some sports, like smokers, are heavily dependent on tobacco sponsorship", adding that "we will therefore give them time and help to reduce their dependency on the weed and replace it with sponsorship from more benign sources". This was terrible news for a wide range of sports benefiting from tobacco sponsorship, with events including the Embassy world championships for darts and snooker, the Benson & Hedges international angling competition, the Benson & Hedges cups for cricket and ice hockey, the Alfred Dunhill golf cup, the Rugby League Silk Cut Challenge cup, and a range of motor racing teams such as Williams, sponsored by Rothmans to the tune of £15m a year. The ruling affected sentiment towards the Formula One flotation, which was revving up for the green light at the time.

There are plenty of things which could go wrong, but by far the largest potential fly in the ointment is hooliganism. For now it seems to have been eradicated, thanks to better stadia, higher prices, clever policing, and a change in football culture, but it could rear its ugly head again. If it were to do so, then many of the strides made by the game over the past twenty years could be wiped out at a stroke. Attendances would diminish as middle-class fans and families began to stay away, football would lose its hard-won social acceptance, overseas stars would leave, and sponsorship cash would evaporate. Fans would again be scared to display their teams colours. This is the one factor above all others which could destroy the sector for investors. If hooliganism returned, the repercussions would be felt throughout the sports industry, and authorities will have to guard against complacency. It is all too easy to assume that the problem has been solved, when there is a possibility that it has merely been shelved. The truth is that it still exists, fairly close to home. In April 1997 the Dutch government announced new measures to tackle football violence when a fan died after gangs from Ajax Amsterdam and Feyenoord Rotterdam clashed on a day when the teams were not even playing. A news report from Reuters on the incident referred to "general agreement that soccer hooliganism was on the increase". British football has come a long way since a *Sunday Times* article in the mid-1980s described it as "a slum sport watched by slum people in slum stadiums", but a watchful eye will need to be kept on the convalescing patient to guard against a relapse.

THE FINAL WHISTLE

Overall, it is difficult to see the sports sector contracting. Greater media opportunities stimulated by advances in technology mean that audiences can watch more sport than ever before, and the demand feeds upon itself. Just as hooliganism and tragedy caused a vicious circle in the 1970s and 1980s, so the late 1990s and early 2000s should see a continuance of the virtuous circle which has already begun. Success rears success, and the great public interest in sport generates a huge amount of business, media coverage, and new strands of commercial enterprise. Take replica club shirts as an example. It is the performance of the team which first stimulates the interest, which is then taken up by the shirt manufacturers. They conduct their own advertising, which creates more demand, and as sales take off, so other fans join the trend and buy from retailers, who in turn devote more shop space to the shirts. The club derives an increasing stream of revenue from the merchandising, which allows them to reinvest in playing staff to keep up the good perfomances, thereby completing the circle.

The expansion of sports shares in the UK is a part of that virtuous circle. Companies decide to come to the stockmarket for a reason, after all. Retailers want stockmarket cash to expand their chains and sell more sporting goods; clubs use the cash to buy better players and improve stadia. The extra cash coming into sport is used to create more demand, more interest, more media coverage, and finally, more revenue. When competitors see these benefits, they join the trend, hence the steady flow of football clubs and fitness clubs coming to the market. The result for investors is that there are more sports shares from which to choose, and more potentially profitable investments.

Having read this book, you should be better equipped to score a few winners and avoid too many own goals when investing. Just as no cricketer will score a century in every innings, so you will not always make profits, but your training should at least make you fit to meet the challenge.

APPENDIX ONE – SOURCES OF INFORMATION

Aerofilms Guide: Football Grounds, 4th Edition
Ian Allan Mail Order
10-14 Eldon Way
Lineside Estate
Littlehampton
West Sussex BN17 7HE

Bloomberg
39-45 Finsbury Square
London EC2A 1PX

Brewin Dolphin & Co Limited
5 Giltspur Street
London EC1A 9BD

Charters on Charting
B T Batsford Ltd
PO Box 4
Braintree
Essex CM7 7QY

City Index Limited
Cardinal Court
23 Thomas More Street
London E1 9YY

Covered Warrants Alert newsletter
The McHattie Group
Clifton Heights
Triangle West
Bristol BS8 1EJ

Edinburgh Financial Publishing
3rd Floor
124/5 Princes Street
Edinburgh EH2 4BD

Greig Middleton & Co Limited
66 Wilson Street
London EC2A 2BL

The Hamlyn Guide to Football Collectables by Duncan Chilcott
Reed Consumer Books Ltd
81 Fulham Road
London SW3 6RB

How to Make a Killing in the AIM by Michael Walters
B T Batsford Ltd
PO Box 4
Braintree
Essex CM7 7QY

ICV Limited
Skandia House
23 College Hill
Cannon Street
London EC4R 2RA

IG Index plc
1 Warwick Row
London SW1E 5ER

Harold Nass Esq
Keith Bayley Rogers & Co
Ebbark House
93-95 Borough High Street
London Bridge
London SE1 1NL

Internet addresses:
http://www.londonstockex.co.uk
http://www.steelers.co.uk
http://www.cobragolf.com
http://www.bba.co.uk
http://www.raceweb.com/newbury
http://www.williamhill.co.uk

Kick Off Official Supporters Guide
Sidan Press
4 Denbigh Mews
Denbigh Street
London SW1V 2HQ

Ladbroke Sporting Spreads
Imperial House
Imperial Drive
Rayners Lane
Harrow
Middlesex HA2 7JW

Momentum UK Limited
140 Brompton Road
London SW3 1HY

Nomura International plc
Nomura House
1 St Martin's-le-Grand
London EC1A 4NP

Reuters Limited
85 Fleet Street
London EC4P 4AJ

Singer & Friedlander Football Fund
21 New Street
Bishopsgate
London EC2M 4HR

Small Company Selector newsletter
The McHattie Group
Clifton Heights
Triangle West
Bristol BS8 1EJ

Sporting Index Limited
Gateway House
Milverton Street
London SE11 4AP

Sports Shares newsletter
The McHattie Group
Clifton Heights
Triangle West
Bristol BS8 1EJ

Colin T Smart Esq
Walkers, Crips, Weddle, Beck plc
Sophia House
76-80 City Road
London EC1Y 2BJ

APPENDIX TWO – SPORTS SHARES AND THEIR ADDRESSES

Allied Leisure plc (bowling centres)
Stock Exchange Code: ALR
Tower Park
Poole
Dorset BH12 4NU

Arena Leisure plc (Lingfield Park racecourse)
Stock Exchange Code: n/a
8 Baker Street
London W1M 1DA

The Arsenal Football Club plc (football club)
Stock Exchange Code: traded on OFEX
Arsenal Stadium
Avenell Road
Highbury
London N5 1BU

Ashurst Technology plc (metal alloys for bats)
Stock Exchange Code: AHR
Clarendon House
2 Church Street
Hamilton HM11
Bermuda

Aston Villa plc (football club)
Stock Exchange Code: ASV
Villa Park
Birmingham B6 6HE

Birmingham City plc (football club)
Stock Exchange Code: BMC
St Andrews Stadium
Birmingham B9 4NH

Blacks Leisure Group plc (sportswear)
Stock Exchange Code: BSLA
Unit 3
Stephenson Industrial Estate
Washington
Tyne & Wear NE37 3HR

Brands Hatch Leisure plc (motor racing circuits)
Stock Exchange Code: BHL
Brands Hatch Circuit
Fawkham
Longfield
Kent DA3 8NG

Brent Walker Group plc (betting)
Stock Exchange Code: BWL
53-54 Brook's Mews
London W1Y 2NY

Bridgend Group plc (sports & leisure clubs)
Stock Exchange Code: BGDG
Thompson house
20-22 Curtain Road
London EC2A 3NQ

British Bloodstock Agency plc (horses)
Stock Exchange Code: BSK
Queensberry House
High Street
Newmarket
Suffolk CB8 9BD

Brunswick Corp (boats and bowling balls)
Stock Exchange Code: BC
1 North Field CT
Lake Forest IL 60045
United States of America

British Sky Broadcasting Group plc (television coverage)
Stock Exchange Code: BSY
6 Centaurs Business Park
Grant Way
Isleworth
Middlesex TW7 5QD

BS Group plc (greyhound racing)
Stock Exchange Code: BSU
Eastgate House
Eastville
Bristol BS5 6NW

Carlisle Group plc (possible shell for Nottingham Forest)
Stock Exchange Code: CLE
6 Carlos Place
London W1Y 5AE

Caspian Group plc (football club)
Stock Exchange Code: CSP
106 Gloucester Place
London W1H 3DB

CCI Holdings plc (manufacture of clay pigeons)
Stock Exchange Code: CCI
5 Priors Haw Road
Corby
Northants NN17 5JG

Celtic plc (football club)
Stock Exchange Code: CCP
95 Kerrydale Street
Glasgow G40 3RE

Charlton Athletic plc (football club)
Stock Exchange Code: CLO
The Valley
Floyd Road
London SE7 8BL

Chelsea Village plc (football club)
Stock Exchange Code: CAV
Stamford Bridge Grounds
Fulham Road
London SW6 1HS

Chepstow Racecourse plc (racecourse)
Stock Exchange Code: CRC
17 Walsh Street
Chepstow
Gwent NP6 5YH

Chrysalis Group plc (sports TV producer)
Stock Exchange Code: CHS
The Chrysalis Building
Bramley Road
London W10 6SP

Claremont Garments Holdings plc (sportswear)
Stock Exchange Code: CAG
1 Stephenson Road
Peterlee
County Durham SR8 5AX

Clubhaus plc (golf courses)
Stock Exchange Code: CHA
Ixworth House
37 Ixworth Place
London SW3 3QH

Clubpartners International plc (golf & country clubs)
Stock Exchange Code: CLB
Lambourne Golf Club
Dropmore Road
Burnham
Buckinghamshire SL1 8NF

Eagles plc (rugby league club)
Stock Exchange Code: EGL
Stadium Corner
824 Attercliffe Road
Sheffield S9 3RS

English National Investment Company plc (stake in Rangers FC)
Stock Exchange Code: ENI
3 Finsbury Avenue
London EC2M 2PA

Fitness First plc (health & fitness clubs)
Stock Exchange Code: FTF
51 Queens Park
South Drive
Bournemouth
Dorset BH8 9BJ

GlycoSport plc (energy drinks for sport)
Stock Exchange Code: traded on OFEX
14 Oxford Court
Bishopsgate
Manchester M2 3WQ

Grampian Holdings plc (sportswear and goods)
Stock Exchange Code: GRMP
Stag House
Castlebank Street
Glasgow G11 6DY

Hawtin plc (sports equipment & textiles)
Stock Exchange Code: HTI
Ocean Buildings
Bute Crescent
Cardiff CF1 6RT

Hay & Robertson plc (sportswear)
Stock Exchange Code: HAY
36 Heriot Row
Edinburgh EH3 6ES

Heart of Midlothian plc (football club)
Stock Exchange Code: HTM
Tynecastle Park
Gorgie Road
Edinburgh EH11 2NL

Hi-Tec Sports plc (sportswear)
Stock Exchange Code: HTS
Hi-Tec House
Aviation Way
Southend-on-Sea
Essex SS2 6GH

IMS Group plc (sports telephone lines)
Stock Exchange Code: IMS
15 Mark Lane
Leeds LS1 8LB

John David Sports plc (sportswear retailer)
Stock Exchange Code: JD
Unit P14 Parklands
Heywood Distribution Park
Pilsworth Road
Heywood
Lancashire OL10 2TT

JJB Sports plc (sportswear retailer)
Stock Exchange Code: JJB
Martland Park
Challenge Way
Wigan WN5 0LD

Just Group plc (Wembley Sportsmaster toys)
Stock Exchange Code: JUS
Wye House
Granby Road
Bakewell
Derbyshire DE45 1ES

Ladbroke Group plc (sports betting)
Stock Exchange Code: LADB
Chancel House
Neasden Lane
London NW10 2XE

Lady in Leisure plc (fitness clubs)
Stock Exchange Code: LLG
Units 15 & 16
Kingston House
Kingston Park Centre
Newcastle Upon Tyne NE3 2FP

Loftus Road plc (QPR football & Wasps rugby)
Stock Exchange Code: LFT
Hanover House
14 Hanover Square
London W1R 0BE

London & Edinburgh Publishing plc (sports magazines)
Stock Exchange Code: LEP
Suffolk House
Whitfield Place
London W1P 5SF

Manchester United plc (football club)
Stock Exchange Code: MNU
Old Trafford
Manchester M16 0RA

Millwall Holdings plc (football club)
Stock Exchange Code: MWH
The Den
Zamba Road
London SE16 3LN

Newbury Racecourse plc (racecourse)
Stock Exchange Code: traded on OFEX
The Racecourse
Newbury
Berkshire RG14 7NZ

Newcastle United plc (football club)
Stock Exchange Code: NCU
St James' Park
Newcastle upon Tyne NE1 4ST

Pentland Group plc (sportswear)
Stock Exchange Code: PND
Pentland Centre
Lakeside Squires Lane
Finchley
London N3 2QL

PGA European Tour Courses plc (golf courses)
Stock Exchange Code: PGA
Calder House
1 Dover Street
London W1X 3PJ

Preston North End plc (football club)
Stock Exchange Code: PNE
Deepdale
Preston PR1 6RU

The Rangers Football Club plc (football club)
Stock Exchange Code: traded on OFEX
Ibrox Stadium
Glasgow G51 2XD

Regent Inns plc (snooker & sports bars)
Stock Exchange Code: REG
Northway house
1379 High Road
Whetstone
London N20 9LP

Robert H Lowe plc (sportswear)
Stock Exchange Code: LWE
The Roldane Mills
Mill Green
Congleton
Cheshire CW12 1JQ

Sanctuary Leisure plc (leisure centres)
Stock Exchange Code: traded on OFEX
The Sanctuary
Denbigh North Leisure
V7 Saxon Street
Milton Keynes MK1 1SA
Bucks

Seton Healthcare Group plc (sportswear)
Stock Exchange Code: SHA
Tubiton House
Oldham OL1 3HS

Sheffield United plc (football club)
Stock Exchange Code: SUT
Bramall Lane
Sheffield S2 4SU

Snakeboard plc (extreme sports)
Stock Exchange Code: SKE
Fairfax House
Fulwood Place
Gray's Inn
London WC1V 6UB

Southampton Leisure Holdings plc (football club)
Stock Exchange Code: SOO
145 Milton Road
Southampton SO15 2XH

Stanley Leisure plc (horse racing betting)
Stock Exchange: SLY
Stanley House
4/12 Marybone
Liverpool L3 2BY

Sunderland plc (football club)
Stock Exchange: SUA
Roker Park
Sunderland SR6 9SW

Sunleigh plc (golf & sailing products)
Stock Exchange Code: SNLG
Station Works
Long Buckby
Northampton NN6 7PF

Taylor Woodrow plc (builders – sports stands)
Stock Exchange Code: TWOD
4 Dunraven Street
London W1Y 3FG

Thomas Potts plc (potential shell for Nottingham Forest)
Stock Exchange Code: THP
Unit 6   Shenval Estate
Templefields
Harlow
Essex CM20 2BD

Tottenham Hotspur plc (football club)
Stock Exchange Code: TTNM
748 High Road
Tottenham
London N17 0AP

Vardon plc (leisure clubs)
Stock Exchange Code: VDN
5 Lower Belgrave Street
London SW1W 0NR

Waterfall Holdings plc (snooker clubs & fishing)
Stock Exchange Code: WFH
53/55 High Street
Aldershot
Hampshire GU11 1BY

Whitbread plc (brewers and sports facilities)
Stock Exchange Code: WTB
Chiswell Street
London EC1Y 4SD

Windsor plc (sports insurance)
Stock Exchange Code: WNDR
Lyon House
160-166 Borough High Street
London SE1 1JR

Wembley plc (football stadium)
Stock Exchange Code: WMY
The Wembley Stadium
Wembley HA9 0DW

West Bromich Albion plc (football club)
Stock Exchange Code: WBA
The Tom Silk Building
Halfords Lane
West Bromwich
West Midlands B71 4BR

Young (H) Holdings plc (sportswear & retail)
Stock Exchange Code: YON
Dominion House
Kennelside
Newbury
BerkshireRG14 5PX

Zetters Group plc (football pools)
Stock Exchange Code: ZTTR
86-88 Clerkenwell Road
London EC1P 1ZS

APPENDIX THREE – SPECIAL OFFER FOR NEWSLETTER

SP⚽RTS SHARES

The UK's only guide to companies in the sports field

The McHattie Group   Clifton Heights
Triangle West   Bristol   BS8 1EJ
Tel: 0117 925 8882   Fax: 0117 925 4441

COACHING YOU TO PICK THE WINNERS

You have read *How to Invest in Sports Shares,* you now know how to get started and you want to take the plunge, but you still require a regular source of independent advice. Look no further. **Sports Shares** is the only monthly newsletter devoted to this fast-growing sector of the UK stockmarket. It covers companies managing football clubs, manufacturing sportswear, running stadia, publishing programmes, operating the football pools, owning horses, building golf courses, and even making clay pigeons.

Sports Shares introduces you to the full range of companies trading in the sports field and aims to alert you to the many profitable investments available.

Sports shares are among the top-performers on the stock market, and with a queue of football clubs and other companies waiting for a listing, there should be plenty of action to come.

Every month, **Sports Shares** highlights new issue opportunities and gives you the news, insight and analysis you need to pick the winners.

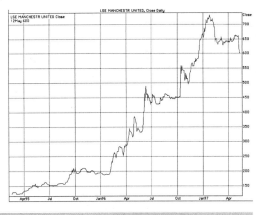

TOP PERFORMING SPORTS SHARES OVER THE YEAR

English National Inv Co	+278.33%	Fitness First*	+ 74.03%
Blacks Leisure	+192.56%	Waterfall Holdings	+ 72.55%
Hay & Robertson	+116.54%	Southampton Leisure	+ 66.04%
West Bromwich Albion*	+ 80.00%	JJB Sport	+ 63.99%
Chelsea Village	+ 75.40%	CCI Holdings	+ 54.66%

* since issue.   All figures are mid-price to mid-price; dealing costs and spreads ignored. Change for year to 4/6/97.

SUBSCRIBE NOW TO SAVE £20 - SEE OVER FOR DETAILS

Sports Shares has a wide range of sources and other forms of information unavailable to private investor

- **continuous contact with all sports companies**
- **company visits and research trips**
- **sophisticated computer programs which track the market, highlighting shares on the move**
- **automatic capture of all relevant Stock Exchange announcements as they happen**
- **industry surveys**
- **analyst research reports**
- **interviews with key industry players**

ALL of this information is used for one purpose only - to provide **Sports Shares** subscribers with unique insight into the prospects for profitable investment in this exciting sector.

SUBSCRIBE NOW AND SAVE 33%

As a special introduction to *How to Invest in Sports Shares* readers, we are offering a reduction 33% on the normal subscription price. Pay just £39.99 for a full year's information and advice. soon as you subscribe, you will be sent an acknowledgement of your order, followed shortly afte wards by the first of your twelve monthly newsletters. **All you need to do complete your address and bank details on the coupon below. Simp return the coupon to us - you do not need to send cash (except oversea please add £12).**

Sports Shares is published by The McHattie Group, Clifton Heights, Triangle West, Bristol, BS8 1EJ. Telephone: 0 925 8882. Fax: 0117 925 4441. Regulated by the Personal Investment Authority. Warning: investors should speculate using money they cannot afford to lose. Because this investment may go down in value as well as up, may not get back the full amount invested. The newsletter gives general advice only, and the investments mentio may not be suitable for any individual. Investors should seek appropriate professional advice if any points are uncle

---

KICK OFF YOUR SUBSCRIPTION WITH THIS £20 SAVING!

YES I wish to take advantage of your special offer and have completed the details below. I understand that will pay just £39.99 this year and £59.99 each year thereafter. **(Please print and return the form to us)**

Mr/Mrs/Miss/Dr ....

Address ....

....

....

Postcode ....

Date ....

Signature ....

To (your bank) .... Bank plc.

Address ....

....

....

Current Account no. ....

Branch sort code ....

Please pay to National Westminster Bank plc (50-41-10 1 Abbey Road, London, NW10 7RA, for the credit of TH McHATTIE GROUP, account number 53400720 the su of £39.99 on receipt of this order and thereafter £59.99 c the same date each year until countermanded by me.

HISS/97

Please return to: Sports Shares, The McHattie Group, Clifton Heights, Triangle West, Bristol, BS8 1EJ

INDEX

INDEX

Windsor insurance brokers 14, 66

winter sports goods 114-117

Woods, Tiger 112, 114, 124-125

workers' freedom of movement 27

Zambia 122

Zetters Group 65, 92

Zola 30